The East Pakistan Tragedy

The
East Pakistan
Tragedy

L F RUSHBROOK WILLIAMS

DRAKE PUBLISHERS INC   NEW YORK
381 Park Avenue South
New York, N.Y. 10016

VERSO

ISBN 87749-246-8

954.92
W724e

Published in 1972 by
Drake Publishers Inc
381 Park Avenue South
New York, N.Y. 10016

72-4007

Printed in the United States

Contents

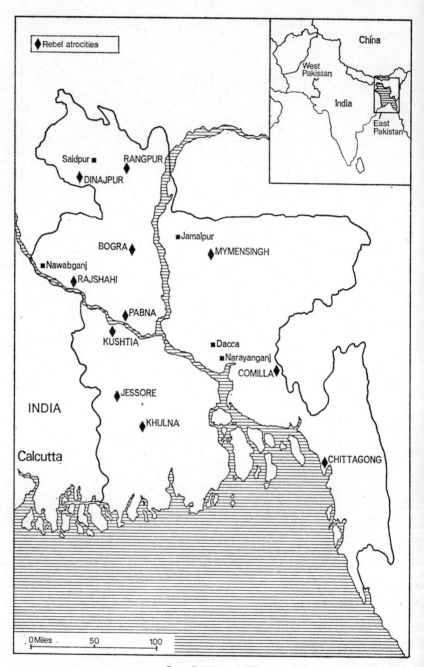

East Pakistan 1971

Timetable of events

1970

NOVEMBER   Disastrous cyclone and tidal wave in East Pakistan delta cause thousands of deaths

DECEMBER   Zulfikar Bhutto wins election in West Pakistan and Sheikh Mujibur Rahman in East Pakistan

1971

MARCH 2   President Yahya Khan postpones the first meeting of the Assembly

MARCH 4   East Pakistan paralyzed by a general strike

MARCH 6   Riots develop into organized revolt

MARCH 19   Sheikh Mujibur Rahman rejects President Yahya Khan's offer to set up commission of enquiry into clashes

MARCH 26   President's attempts to end conflict fail and shooting breaks out all over Dacca

APRIL 14   Resistance crumbles as President Yahya Khan's troops advance

MAY 11   All serious resistance ends

JUNE 11   President Yahya Khan offers amnesty to all who return

JULY 3   Planters return to estates

DECEMBER 13-22   By-elections to be held in East Pakistan

DECEMBER 20   Constitution to be announced by President Yahya Khan

DECEMBER 27   National Assembly to be convened and followed by the formation of a civilian Government

Acknowledgements

I must express my great obligation to many officials, both in the civilian and the defence services of Pakistan, who gave us so much of their time and answered my questions so patiently. But I must make clear that they are not responsible for what I have written. Any judgments expressed are my own.

Also I am most grateful to our many friends in East and West Pakistan who talked to us so freely and admitted us to their confidence. I hope that I have not abused it.

Foreword

There are certain aspects of the tragic events in East Pakistan which I find very puzzling. Human suffering, particularly on a mass-scale, is always heart-breaking; as an elderly historian who has been studying and writing about the Indo-Pakistani subcontinent since 1914, it has been my fate to see much of it. I hope and believe that such harrowing experiences have not made me callous; but I think that they have enabled me to set the East Pakistan tragedy in something like a true perspective. Refugee and famine camps are terrible; the unfortunates who inhabit them have invariably fearful sufferings to relate and bitter blame to assign to those whom they regard – whether Governments or private individuals – as responsible for their misfortunes. But alas! such camps are nothing new, even if their impact upon those who visit one for the first time is shattering.

It seems to me that there is something very odd about the way in which the East Pakistan tragedy has been presented to the outside world. As a historian, I can find plenty of parallels in the past to what has happened; but in the past, such happenings have never been made the occasion for violent attacks upon a particular Government. The mass· and individual tragedies accompanying the partition in 1947 and 1948 between India and West Pakistan were at least as poignant as anything that has happened in East Pakistan in 1971; the numbers affected were certainly no smaller. Yet at that time, no foreign country threatened the Governments of either India or Pakistan with dire sanctions, economic or political; it was assumed that each was doing its best under difficult circumstances. Again, India's occupation by armed might of the most fertile portions of the former State of Jammu and Kashmir, certainly against the will of the majority of the population, aroused little emotion outside Kashmir and Pakistan; and India's skilful torpedo-ing of the plebiscite planned to ascertain the real wishes of the Kashmiris left world opinion largely unmoved. No British Members of Parliament, no Members of Congress, demanded action against India; there were no processions in the streets of London or Washington in support of Kashmiri claims to self-determination.

To come to more recent times. No foreign country, no corres-pondent of a foreign newspaper, criticised India's handling of the results of such natural catastrophes as the successive floods and droughts which have brought tragedy to millions of her people; it was assumed, perfectly correctly, that her Government were doing all that lay in their power to afford succour and relief.

Yet contrast this with the impassioned denunciations of the Pakistan Government for the alleged shortcomings in their handling of the consequences of the two natural catastrophes which devas-tated parts of East Pakistan at the end of 1970. From much of what was said and written, an impartial observer might be pardoned for assuming that both tragedies had been brought about by an evil conspiracy between President Yahya Khan and the Clerk of the Weather. The important facts that meteorological warning was duly given – unfortunately, such warnings are necessarily so frequent in the cyclone areas that they are too often ignored – and that the armed forces worked day and night to bring relief, and can proudly claim that not a single life was lost through lack of food or medical supplies after the force of the cyclone was spent, were ignored both locally and by the outside world.

Nor is this all. The widespread and inhuman massacres of men, women and children by Awami League militants during their brief reign of terror in March and April 1971, although factually reported by several foreign correspondents, aroused comparatively little attention throughout the world. Yet this was true genocide in the worst sense of the word. Some of the victims were West Pakistanis, many of whom had been settled for years; the majority were Bihari Muslims, who had come to East Pakistan at the time of Partition, and had lived there for more than two decades, peaceably and trustingly. Ironically enough, some of those who were brutally murdered were Bengali by race, who had come from such places as Rangoon, Bombay and Calcutta to live in a Muslim-majority land. In the eyes of their murderers their offence was threefold; they did not support an independent 'Bangla Desh' even though many of them had voted for the maximum local autonomy for East Pakistan which was the main platform of the Awami League's election programme; they did not speak the local patois of Bengali; above all, their industry and hard work had made them relatively prosperous – the fact that this prosperity was shared by the locality in which they lived and that they gave employment to many was overlooked. The total butcher's bill for those few terrible weeks will never be known; but from the mass graves which the Army found when at last it was able to fan out from its stations and restore order, the numbers murdered cannot be less than 120,000 and may be far higher, as many corpses were just thrown into the rivers and carried away. It was these mass-killings, rather than the actions of the Army, which set in motion the exodus across the Indian border, although no doubt some of the refugees, particularly the committed 'Bangla Desh' partisans, feared lest they might be denounced for their crimes to the authorities when order was restored. Many consciences, too, must have been uneasy about the looting, arson, and terrorism which, even if they had taken no part in them, they had done little or nothing to stop.

There is some evidence, too, of the deliberate spread of false rumours about the fearful vengeance which the Army was about to exact when it arrived. The joint effect of all this was to set in motion a wave of mass-panic which carried millions of frightened people across the Indian border. Yet the world has been made to believe that it was the Army, not the Bengali mobs, that was guilty of genocide. Admittedly, when the Army was fired upon, it acted with sternness, but its aim was to restore order with the minimum loss of life. It is surely more humane to clear road-blocks and snipers' nests by using tracer bullets to start fires from which the occupants can escape, rather than to shoot them down. No doubt, even in a highly-disciplined Army, proud of its British traditions, as is the Army of Pakistan, individuals occasionally get out of hand, especially when they are confronted with the corpses of murdered relatives and hear the sorrowful wails of the survivors. What the Army found in several places can only be compared with what British soldiers found in 1857 at the Well of Cawnpore – the photographic evidence is indescribably gruesome. All such cases of individual vengeance were promptly brought to a court-martial.

Moreover, from the recorded voices of widows and orphans it is clear that their relatives were the victims of mob violence – beaten to death with cudgels and finished off with knives. An Army does not execute vengeance like this. Even so, the Pakistan Army, and President Yahya Khan himself, have been pilloried by world opinion as brutal repressors of a praiseworthy campaign of national self-determination.

This line of reasoning did not convince me, from my personal knowledge of local conditions and of the people involved. During three visits to East and West Pakistan within the space of a few months, I tried to find out the facts. This book is the result.

As this book goes to Press, the risk of open hostilities between India and Pakistan appears increasingly serious. Should this occur, the progress of Pakistan towards constitutional Government may be further delayed, and the consequences to both countries may well be disastrous in other directions. Every friend of India and Pakistan must pray that such a catastrophe may be avoided. However this may be, the facts set out in this narrative will, I hope, assist its readers to judge the rights and wrongs of the quarrel for themselves.

Finally it is worth remembering that (1) Pakistan accepted U Thant's proposal of July 19, 1971 to station UN observers on the borders to assist in the repatriation of refugees. India refused. (2) Pakistan proposed that a general offices committee drawn from the Security Council should visit the areas of tension. Neither was this accepted. (3) Pakistan offered a mutual withdrawal of troops to agreed distances away from the borders to relieve tension. India refused. (4) President Yahya Khan repeatedly offered to meet Mrs. Gandhi to discuss the East Pakistan situation. No meeting has taken place.

L. F. Rushbrook Williams.

Chapter **1**   East Pakistan: The Legacies of the Past

S O U R C E S *Imperial Gazetteer of India, 1906 edition, vols vii and xii*
Oxford History of India, 3rd edition 1958
Ian Stephens Pakistan
Rushbrook Williams The State of Pakistan

Some knowledge of the past is essential if the present problems of East Pakistan are to be understood. This area has a long history, readily distinguishable from that of other parts of the ancient land of Bengal; but until quite recently, it has enjoyed few opportunities to rule itself. For centuries, the mass of the population – which today forms the majority of the people of Pakistan – has been Muslim; but even in Mughal times, few of the nobility and of the large landholders held that faith; the men of mark were mainly Hindus. Even now, the old country manor-houses, from which Hindu squires for so long controlled the lives of their Muslim tenants-at-will are still to be seen, though ruined and deserted by their former owners. But early in the present century things began to change; the interests of the Muslims found some champions in a small educated urban middle-class which was gradually forming. Yet even these were mostly graduates of the University of Calcutta, and they preferred to live in the vigorous surroundings of that great city, then the almost undisputed leader of Indian social, political and economic life, rather than in the somnolent backwaters of East Pakistan. Yet, the stirrings of Muslim nationalism were there; it was in Dacca that the foundations of the Muslim League, which eventually created Pakistan under Mr. Jinnah's inspiration and guidance, were first laid in 1906.

At that time, the area was entirely agricultural, densely populated even then, with a pitiably low standard of living. Only one crop of any commercial importance – jute – was grown. Nature was both kind and cruel; the land was fertile and enormously well-watered;

but because of the deltaic character of most of the countryside, annual floods and recurring devastating cyclones exposed large tracts to appalling disasters and frightful famines and epidemics. British records tell of such terrible catastrophes as that of 1876, when most of Backergunge and its adjoining districts were submerged to a depth of from 10 to 45 feet. The loss of life could not be reckoned but it is known that 50,000 people died in the cholera epidemic which followed. Communications between different parts of the land were slow and difficult; networks of waterways made roads impossible except for short local stretches. During the rainy season each village, raised upon a mound above the normal flood level, was waterbound, cut off from its neighbours except by boat. There were very few towns of any size; even Dacca, the seat of goverment since Mughal times, had a population of only 90,000 – mainly Hindu, with a few town houses of local magnates, a Government office or two, and some ancient and famous mosques. Chittagong, the only possible deep-water port, had few facilities, was badly silted up, and could not accommodate vessels of any size. In short, the entire area of what is now East Pakistan remained remote, undeveloped and neglected. More important still, the outlook of its people, like their opportunities, remained provincial, narrow, and self-centred.

Between 1905 and 1911, there came the promise of a change. In the former year the then Viceroy, Lord Curzon, decided that the enormous province of Bengal was administratively unwieldy, and that the neglect which had for centuries over-shadowed its eastern regions could no longer be tolerated. He established a new Province, called Eastern Bengal and Assam, with its capital at Dacca. For the next few years, steady progress was made in education, communications and the other concomitants of growth. Dacca was adorned with handsome buildings, including colleges and a High Court. A Governor took up his residence; a provincial Secretariat was established; judges were appointed. For the first time in centuries, the land that is now East Pakistan became a separate entity, with its own administrative establishment devoted to the promotion of its own interests. Unfortunately, all this was too good to last. Lord Curzon's move was hotly denounced by the educated classes, mainly Hindu, of Calcutta and of what is now West Bengal. He was accused of striking a blow at the entire nationalist movement – of which Bengal had been for some time the spearhead

– by splitting the Presidency and setting up a Muslim-majority Province. Agitation, both violent and non-violent continued unabated. It achieved its objective. In 1911 the arrangement was revoked; Curzon's administrative goal was approached by another path; a new Province of Bihar and Orissa was set up; the old Chief Commissionership of Assam was revived; and Eastern areas were once more merged into Bengal. The people of what is now East Pakistan were dismayed and resentful, regarding the reversal of British policy as a triumph for the Hindu intellectuals of Calcutta and a defeat for Muslim aspirations. When I first toured the country in 1918, in the entourage of Sir Henry Wheeler, then Revenue Member of the Governor of Bengal's Council, feelings were still very bitter. The people felt that they had been let down by the British to placate the Hindus; they had lost a Government of their own. The memory of this rankled for years; it was a powerful factor in that determination to stand on their own legs which lay at the root of Mr. Jinnah's success in his campaign for the establishment of a Muslim National Home. I could understand their dismay. Progress had been halted; Dacca was forlorn, with its brave new buildings crumbling into obsolescence and its Muslim population relapsing into their former apathy.

It is thus scarcely a matter for surprise that at a time when certain sections of the Muslim community in the west were still doubtful about the expediency, and even the possibility, of establishing the kind of Muslim National Home for which Iabal had pleaded and Mr. Jinnah was working, the people of East Bengal – at least the Muslim masses – did not hesitate. They became his most enthusiastic supporters. Yet there was a marked difference between the ways in which West Pakistan and East Pakistan respectively came into existence. East Pakistan witnessed none of the fearful massacres and pitiful migrations which accompanied Partition on the Western side. This was more remarkable because there were far more Hindus living in the East than in the West. Not only so; these Hindus held all the more important positions. Most of the Government Officers, most of the lawyers, practically all the large landholders were Hindus. They dominated finance, commerce and such industry as there was – which was very little. They monopolized the professions of medicine and teaching. And the Muslims had become so accustomed to this situation that it aroused little resentment among them. The dependence of East Pakistan's entire economic and administrative structure upon the educated Hindu element became a factor of cardinal importance when Pakistan became an independent country.

After partition, very large numbers of Hindus occupying key-positions decided to migrate to West Bengal. They were under no compulsion to do so; but Calcutta had always been their spiritual home, and they realised that their virtual monopoly of wealth, power and influence was bound to come to an end with the emergence of Pakistan. The migration was entirely peaceful; real property which could not be taken away remained in their owner-ship until the era of agrarian reforms. A large town house, with its contents, was perfectly safe in the custody of one old woman; not a single Hindu temple or Sikh gurdwara or Buddhist shrine was violated. For quite a time, Hindus who had sent their families to Calcutta continued to practise in the professions, transferring their salaries without hindrance. It was only when they found this arrangement inconvenient that they left, without any compulsion from local authorities who were only too eager to assure them of their safety. The real tragedy was that there were few educated Muslims to take their place. Hardly any natives of what is now East Pakistan had entered the former All-India services; those that had done so remained in subordinate positions. In lesser degree, the same thing was true of the Provincial Services. Hardly any East Pakistanis held commissioned rank in the armed Services; the profession of arms was never popular among people of Bengali race, and British experiments in this direction during the First World War were not encouraging, although some of the hardy seamen of the Chittagong region – formerly notorious for piracy – had entered the Indian Navy. Most unfortunately, the Muslims who migrated from India to East Pakistan – the majority came from Bihar – were mainly of the cultivating and small shopkeeping classes. They could not fill the gap left by the Hindus. Further, those Hindus who decided to remain in East Pakistan – some nine millions in number – were mostly of the low income group; they could not fill the gap left by the departure of the educated elements of their community.

The result of this situation was that there were very few people left in East Pakistan who possessed the kind of experience needed to administer the country or to promote its economy. Centuries of virtual control – and it would not be an exaggeration to say centuries of exploitation – by Hindu elements whose cultural and material outlook was that of Calcutta, had deprived the local Muslim community of initiative as well as of expertise. Time was needed to remedy this situation; but in the early days of Pakistan's struggle for existence, time was very short. What could Mr. Jinnah do?

Probably no other Head of State which had recently gained its independence had been called upon to face the difficulties which confronted Quaid-i-Azam. In West Pakistan, the situation was bad enough; but at least he had some trained members of the All-India Services on which to build the administration. Out of the initial confusion, when the Government in Karachi had to carry on with no records, no precedents, no accommodation and scarcely a type-writer, and with millions of homeless and penniless refugees from India to resettle, order gradually emerged. But in East Pakistan there seemed to be almost nothing to build upon in the way of administrative experience or local leadership. Moreover, East and West Pakistan were separated by a thousand miles of potentially hostile territory – for India, from the earliest days of Pakistan's existence, had been hoping eagerly for her neighbour's collapse. Before long, thanks to air travel and radio, the gap between the two parts of Pakistan was bridged at the cost of a few hours of time; but communication of this kind could not be extemporized immediately; and meanwhile the plight of East Pakistan was critical. Her economy was almost entirely based on jute. For many years, this crop had been financed, moved and marketed by Marwari business men from Calcutta; there was not a single jute mill in East Pakistan. After Partition, these Marwaris ceased to come, expecting that the jute cultivators would be compelled to accept absurdly low prices rather than face starvation. By almost super-human exertions, the Government of Pakistan set up a National Bank to finance the crop, and itself built mills to process the jute. Thus the immediate peril was averted, but at the cost of the undying hostility of powerful West Bengal business interests. Further, Mr. Jinnah appointed a good British Governor to East Pakistan, along with some trained men whom he could ill spare.

Mr. Jinnah's charismatic image was so reverenced among the East Pakistanis that they were ready to accept any arrangement which he proposed. But even from the first, they were unhappy about this influx of officials from the western wing. For the most part these officials did not know Bengali; had not Quaid-i-Azam himself insisted that the national language of Pakistan must be Urdu, with English tolerated as a convenience? They were not always tactful in pointing out the administrative inexperience of the people whom they had come to help, the general lack of initiative and the incompetence of some men who had been promoted to positions of authority because no better material was available. The Westerners complained that they were being treated as outsiders by the East Pakistanis, who would neither help themselves nor allow anyone else to help them. They considered the East Pakistanis to be both clannish and incompetent, prouder of being Bengalis than of being Pakistanis, and largely lacking in the new national outlook which Mr. Jinnah was instilling into his countrymen. Looking back on this period, an impartial observer might be justified in holding that these competent, bustling Westerners failed to make adequate allowance for the centuries of exploitation from Calcutta and Greater Bengal which had hindered the emergence of local leadership, discouraged initiative, and afforded few opportunities for the acquisition of expertise in administration. Nor did they appreciate the fact that the East Pakistanis, although virtually excluded from power and responsibility for the management of their own affairs, had found compensation in other directions. Their artists, their poets, and their orators were both numerous and famous; they had enormous pride in their cultural heritage.

The reaction of the East Pakistanis was exactly what might have been expected. They were quite aware that they made up more than half the population of Pakistan, and they knew that their jute crop was then the greatest source of export trade in the entire country, and the principal earner of foreign exchange. They resented the selection of Karachi as the seat of the Central Government, fearing that the people of West Pakistan, being nearer at hand, would be able to exercise a greater influence in national affairs. Moreover the East Pakistanis, with some justice, asserted that they enjoyed a virtual unity of race and culture – leaving aside some small minority tribal elements in such localities as the Chittagong Hill Tracts – which was lacking in West Pakistan, made up as it was of such diverse materials as West Punjab, the North-West Frontier Province, Sind, Baluchistan, the Hill territories and a few Princely States.

Mr. Jinnah was perfectly aware of all this; he lectured both sides sharply for their intolerant attitudes, and insisted that East Pakistanis must be given the opportunity to take their full share in national affairs. He was as good as his word: East Pakistanis enjoyed their moiety of Cabinet and other appointments; while a handful of prominent men of great ability, like the late H. S. Suhrawardy, who had won their spurs in the cut-and-thrust debates in the old Bengal Legislature, quickly made their mark in the new National Assembly of Pakistan. So long as Mr. Jinnah lived, there was little real trouble; but after his death in 1948 the old difficulties emerged again. For the next few years, the East and the West wings were virtually forced into better understanding by the steady hostile pressure which India exerted against Pakistan in both the economic and political fields when her original hopes of an early collapse, leading to an approach by Pakistan to rejoin India were frustrated; but there was a perceptible tendency for East and West Pakistan to develop along different lines. The sheer weight of East Pakistan's superiority in population as well as her fundamental unity of culture and outlook overshadowed the individual elements which made up West Pakistan. Fortunately for the country as a whole, there were plenty of East Pakistanis who were proud of Pakistan, and as their experience grew, they began to take a greater and greater part in national affairs. A convention quickly grew up that if the Head of State – at first the Governor General and after 1956 the President – were a West Pakistani, the Prime Minister must come from the Eastern Wing, and vice versa. Further, when, in order to achieve something like a political balance between the two wings, one of which was superior in population and the other in economic development, the first Constituent Assembly decided that West and East Pakistan should enjoy parity of representation in future National Parliaments, there were few objections from the East Pakistan side. It was felt that Bengali adroitness and Bengali oratory would easily suffice to protect Eastern interests, the more so that the Bengali language now ranked with Urdu as a national medium of communication.

Most unfortunately for the country as a whole, it so happened that the main pre-occupations of the Central Government continued for a number of critical years to be concerned with such matters as Kashmir, the division of the Indus Valley water resources, and other causes of friction with India which concerned East Pakistan only indirectly. But they were of vital interest to West Pakistan, whose problems and outlook thus came to engross a very large share of the Central Government's attention. Moreover, West Pakistan was advancing very fast in the economic sphere; industry, commerce and finance in that Wing soon became the mainstay of the Pakistan Government. With the conspicuous exception of a number of East Pakistani statesmen and leaders of great ability, who played a worthy part in directing the policy of the whole country, most of the people of East Pakistan felt themselves cut off from the main stream of national politics and preferred to concentrate on local affairs. On occasion, they were stirred to indignation by hearing from new waves of Muslim refugees of the difficulties, and from time to time the tragedies – which overtook the Muslim community in different parts of India; for Mr. Nehru's ideal of the Secular State, in which no discrimination was to be made between communities on the grounds of creed or race, was sometimes more honoured in the breach than in the observance, except at the Centre and in the State Capitals. With the growing strength of organizations such as the Jan Singh, which openly worked for the reversal of the 1947 Partition and the reincorporation of Pakistan into *Akhand Bharat* – 'Undivided India' – under Hindu auspices, attacks upon Muslims became more serious and more frequent, in spite of all that the Central Government could do to stop them. But the resentment which such sad happenings excited was far deeper in West than in East Pakistan, where the Muslim majority was well accustomed to living side by side with the quite considerable Hindu minority and had, as a whole fewer causes for resentment against India.

There was a marked tendency in East Pakistan to concentrate upon purely local affairs. Party strife between rival aspirants for power was amazingly bitter, and 'riotous assemblies' were far from uncommon. A very unfortunate feature of political life in East Pakistan has for long been the part played by the student community, members of which were frequently said by ambitious politicians to collect bands of their fellows to demonstrate, to break up the meetings of opposing factions, and generally to terrorise those whom they were ordered to embarrass. Outside influences of this kind naturally had a deleterious effect upon University and College discipline; teaching Staff were frequently threatened with physical violence or kept prisoner in their offices

– a process known as 'gherao-ing' if they set examination papers which the students regarded as too stiff, or failed to pass a high proportion of examinees regardless of standards. Moreover the authorities regulating admissions were pressurized to enroll large numbers of students who were affiliated to such organizations as the Awami ('Freedom') League, and were less interested in university education than in using strong-man tactics against the opponents of those who patronized them. Dacca University, in particular, suffered greatly from all this; I was informed by the University authorities that during 1969-1970, several thousand 'students' had to be admitted, because of political pressures, who had really no claim at all to higher education and no interest in receiving it. In July 1971, a very senior East Pakistan political leader admitted ruefully to me: 'We found the students very useful when we were agitating against the British, but I am afraid that the whole thing has boomeranged back on us!' Needless to say, he was not a supporter of the Awami League.

Leftwing reformist policies have been strong in East Pakistan; and parties rivalled each other in putting forward radical programmes. A good six years before Field Marshal Ayub Khan's administration began to tackle agrarian reform in West Pakistan, the East Pakistan Legislature decided to break up all large landed estates and to fix a maximum holding of thirty acres. This was in 1952; and the original idea was to pay compensation to dispossessed people over a term of years. But in 1956 it was decided to take over all the land by a fixed date. Political in-fighting grew more and more bitter; in 1968 the Speaker of the East Pakistan Legislative Assembly was attacked and his Deputy so badly beaten up that he died. Only on one matter were the bulk of educated Bengalis united; and that was their resentment at the contrast between their own economic condition and the growing prosperity of West Pakistan. It was more palatable to argue that East Pakistan was the victim of 'colonialist exploitation' by West Pakistan than to face the fact that because of past events, or rather, perhaps of non-events, the infra-structure required for economic advance, including capital accumulation, business expertise and industrial initiative was entirely lacking. Over-population was by itself a terrible problem; it was perhaps the most powerful factor in neutralizing the best efforts of successive Governments, local and central, to raise living standards. There were also certain elements in the population, partly Muslim but mainly Hindu, who had never freed themselves from the 'pull' of Calcutta and West Bengal, and were influenced in their outlook by the prevalent Indian wish to see Pakistan break up. Along with discontent, there came a disposition to attribute to West Pakistan the responsibility for everything that was wrong in the Eastern Wing.

As a foreigner, uncommitted to either side, who has visited East Pakistan regularly at frequent intervals for the last sixteen years, this attitude seemed to me worth studying. Quite apart from the statistical evidence which proves that for quite a long time East Pakistan has been drawing from central revenues far more than she contributes to them, my own observations led me to conclude that East Pakistan has made more progress in the economic field in the quarter of a century since Pakistan emerged as an independent State than at any other period in her long history. Leaving aside such great and successful enterprises as the Kaptai Dam, the emergence of Chittagong as a major port, the Chandragona Paper Mills, the Fenugange Fertiliser complex, and the first Steel Mill to be built anywhere in Pakistan – all the result of the central Government's initiative – there has been a notable increase in small private industry. Living standards and per capita income, though still below those prevailing in certain – but by no means all – parts of West Pakistan are steadily if slowly rising. Dacca has grown into a capital city so impressive that any country might be proud of it; with the development of Khul into a great river port, communications by water have been facilitated. Road and rail networks have been greatly extended; internal air services, thanks to the initiative and progressive outlook of Pakistan International Airlines – which run the internal as well as the external air communications of Pakistan – have revolutionized travel between different centres in East Pakistan. The air bus services, with their cheap fares, have done much to make the population air-minded. Yet in spite of the growing benefits which the entire community of East Pakistan has derived from such developments as these, discontent, and criticism of West Pakistan, remains rife among the educated classes, to whom the masses look for leadership. My sense of history tells me that this, however regrettable, is not surprising. A population that is deeply oppressed and sunk in misery shows few signs of restlessness; it lacks the energy. It is when things are beginning to improve, and when the appetite for further and more rapid improvement grows, that restlessness and impatience manifest themselves. And if these emotions are further excited by steady and unremitting, if under-cover, psychological warfare from across the Indian border, they become in time formidable obstacles to the maintenance of order and stability. I doubt very much whether the central Government of Pakistan, considering the very modesty of the means at its disposal, could have done more to bring East Pakistan forward than it has done. Readers who are interested in this question, and who may have come across the carefully-selected statistics upon which the protagonists of an independent East Pakistan ('Bangla Desh') base their accusations of 'colonial-type exploitation' of East by West may care to turn to chapter 7 of this book for facts and figures. These confirm the impression which I, and I am sure other foreign visitors have formed about the remarkable progress which the East Wing has made in recent years. The testimony of resident British, American and Canadian business men, working in East Pakistan on this point should suffice to convince an unbiassed enquirer.

Nor is it only in the economic field that East Pakistan has benefited. From the time of Mr. Jinnah onwards, successive central Governments have tried to ensure that East Pakistanis took their full share in the direction of national affairs. They had a majority of the seats in the National Assembly from the very first, and exercised great influence both in its current business and in the not very successful strivings to frame an agreed constitution – to say nothing of deciding the fate of all too frequently changing administrations. East Pakistanis found careers in the Foreign Service, in which, by 1971, a number had risen to the rank of Ambassador and Counsellor. They entered the Civil Service of Pakistan, the Police Service, and other superior administrative and executive cadres; as was natural, they monopolized the Provincial Services in their own country, and were to be found in considerable numbers in West Pakistan also. The drive to make the fullest possible use of East Pakistani talent was particularly noticeable during the period when Field Marshal Ayub Khan was President; he gave a pledge to East Pakistan that he would not send outsiders to rule her. Governors, G O Cs and Chief Secretaries, were all chosen from East Pakistanis. Half his Presidential Cabinet came from the Eastern Wing; several of the highly-influential Secretaries to the

Central Government were East Pakistanis. East Pakistan recruitment to the armed forces was steadily increased. From the national point of view it was unfortunate, in light of the tragic happenings of 1971, that Pakistan did not follow the British practice of forming class company regiments, but constituted the military and paramilitary forces raised in East Pakistan almost wholly from Bengalis, without much admixture of other ethnic elements. The President was determined to make the East Pakistanis feel that they 'belonged' and were an inseparable part of Pakistan. In the 1962 Constitution, he gave them a high degree of local autonomy; a separate Eastern Wing of the Pakistan Industrial Corporation, which had done so much to bring the whole country forward; a separate Eastern branch of the Water Power and Development Authority; and control of the East Pakistan railway system. Dacca became the second capital of the country, the seat of the National Assembly; its development for its new role took precedence over the President's plans for the building of a new administrative capital at Islamabad, just outside Rawalpindi. He ensured that East Pakistan was given the major share of development grants, that its receipts from central sources exceeded its contribution to them; that the encouragement of new enterprises in the private sphere was more highly subsidized in the East than in the West; that the tax holiday given to foreign capitalists who invested in East Pakistan was longer than that granted to similar investors in the West. In short, he left nothing undone which in his view and that of his advisers could strengthen the links between East and West and convince the East of the tangible advantage of being part of Pakistan.

Looking back on all this with the advantages of hindsight, it is not difficult to escape the conclusion that the results of this policy were not wholly beneficial. It seems to have encouraged a belief, in some East Pakistanis at least, that they were entitled as of right to preferential treatment, independent of individual merit. They tended to resent the fact that they were not promoted over the heads of others who had been longer in the Services or had shown superior capacity. Many of them did very well indeed; but there remained a hard core of men who nursed a grievance and believed that only in an independent East Pakistan would their merits be recognized. This was particularly the case in the armed forces, where seniority plays a large part in deciding promotion; as comparatively late entrants, they felt that their chances of rising to high rank were inferior to their merits. Such men were bitterly if covertly hostile to West Pakistan, convincing themselves that this part of the country controlled and manipulated the central Government, to the disadvantage of the Eastern Wing, and of the people who lived there. Their point of view gained credence because of the fact that the Army, which was mainly recruited from West Pakistan, came prominently to the fore during the periods of martial law administration as a machine for maintaining law and order. It is held even today by the proponents of 'Bangla Desh', who insist that the Central Government has for years been the obedient tool of West Pakistan military interests determined to keep East Pakistan in a subordinate position. I can find no foundation in fact for this theory; on the contrary it seems to me that both Field Marshal Ayub Khan and, perhaps even more notably, General Yahya Khan, have almost leaned over backwards to ensure that the interests of East Pakistan are respected, fostered, and promoted in every possible way.

Under the 1962 Constitution, with its electorate limited to the 'Basic Democrats' themselves chosen by adult suffrage, the political acumen and manipulative powers of the East Pakistan intellectuals came into their own. I myself thought at the time that the system of Basic Democracies, devised by the Field Marshal was an excellent idea; it was founded on the theory that the masses, although they might not be able to understand complicated questions of national policy, were quite competent to choose the best men in the locality to run local affairs; and that the men so chosen, enjoying the trust of their fellows, would form the best kind of electorate that Pakistan could for the moment provide. When my wife and I visited about forty Basic Democracies, half in East and half in West Pakistan, we were impressed by the work that they were doing, and hoped much from the experiment. But as it turned out, we were wrong; the small size of the Basic Democracies, the wide powers that they exercised, and their function as electors both for the office of President and for the National and Provincial Legislatures, proved to be a positive encouragement to corruption of the most flagrant kind. The system fell into disrepute, and this was among the causes of the reaction against Field Marshal Ayub Khan which led him to hand over the country to General Yahya Khan in 1969. But while the 1962 constitution was functioning, East Pakistanis took a prominent part in the National Legislature, and came into prominence as vigorous exponents of the need for Parliamentary government of the type which makes the Executive responsible to the Legislature.

During that period, the Awami League was an inter-wing organization, with an Eastern, a Western, and an All-Pakistan group, as its founder, the late H. S. Suhrawardy, had planned. It was the most powerful party in the Combined Opposition which grew up in the National Assembly. But in 1966 it was disrupted by the action of Sheikh Mujibur Rahman, at that time General Secretary of the East Pakistan Awami League, who produced his famous Six Points. These are set out in detail in Appendix 2; it suffices here to say that they amounted to a demand for a Centre limited to the functions of defence and foreign affairs, and so weakened by devolution of powers of taxation, fiscal control, currency and so forth to the federating units as to be almost incapable of exercising the normal authority of a national government. The Sheikh's action destroyed once and for all the all-Pakistan character of the Awami League; the Western and Central branches went their own ways, while Sheikh Mujibur Rahman returned to Dacca and put forward the Six Points as his personal programme for East Pakistan, commending them to the public in a pamphlet which he wrote himself. Not long afterwards, he was imprisoned and prosecuted for what the Government considered to be his involvement in what was called the Agartala Conspiracy Case – a plan to promote the severance of East Pakistan from the rest of the country with Indian assistance. But when Field Marshal Ayub Khan was vainly trying to reach agreement with the various political parties just prior to his own resignation, the Sheikh was released to take part in the projected conference.

The factor, no doubt, which must eventually have decided the Field Marshal to hand over control to General Yahya Khan and the armed forces, was the outbreak of serious disorders in many urban centres. These were particularly bad in East Pakistan, where mobs of students and industrial employees got completely out of hand, 'gherao-ing' managers and executives of all ranks, putting forward naive and quite impossible demands, and defying the civil authorities. The various political groups tried to outbid each other in appealing to the prevailing fashion, the most violent in speech being the 'National' Awami Party under the lead of the octogenarian Mulla Bashani. The Awami League, under Sheikh

Mujibur Rahman, did not lag far behind. But the ordinary people in East and in West Pakistan soon grew tired of these disorders; and once martial law was imposed, General Yahya Khan encountered little resistance in restoring the rule of law. He proceeded to tackle energetically corruption, labour relations, educated unemployment, University reform, and many other outstanding problems. He refused to become involved in politics, announcing from the first that he was heading only a caretaker administration, and that his main objective was to protect the interests of the whole country, and of everyone in it, pending the time when he could re-establish democratic institutions and hand over control to political leaders elected by the people. From these aims I can testify, of my own knowledge of him and of his policies, gathered in many frank and informal talks, he has never wavered.

S O U R C E S   *President Yahya Khan's broadcasts to the Nation
           in 1969, 1970 and 1971*
           Dawn *(Karachi)*, Pakistan Times *(Rawalpindi)*
           Pakistan Observer *(Dacca)*, The People *(Dacca)*

This book is not a history of President Yahya Khan's administration, still less is it a history of his country; but the situation in East Pakistan cannot be understood without following his intentions for restoring democratic institutions and his plans for carrying these intentions into practice. The materials for such a study are readily available, because of the President's habit of reporting periodically to the people at large through nation-wide broadcasts. These reports were always so frank and forthright that no one could possibly accuse him of ambiguity; he told the country exactly what he was doing or trying to do; the progress that was being made, the difficulties which were being encountered.

Within twenty-four hours of taking over power at the request of Field Marshal Ayub Khan, he announced that his first task was to protect life, liberty and property, to bring back sanity, and to see that the administration resumed its normal function; and that his main aim was the creation of conditions which would make the restoration of constitutional government possible. Political life was not interrupted, although public meetings were temporarily banned in the interests of order. In July 1969 the President called upon all political leaders and political parties to work together to solve the problems confronting the country, at the same time giving a solemn pledge of his Government's complete impartiality towards them all, while adding a warning that any group or party campaigning against the principles of Islam or the solidarity of Pakistan would be dealt with effectively. In this July broadcast he made specific reference to what he termed the justifiable dissatisfaction of the people of East Pakistan at their inability to play their full part in decision-making processes at the national level and in certain important spheres of national activity. He had, he said, taken certain steps to correct this imbalance (the reference, no doubt, was to his decision to ensure that several of the Secretaries in charge of Central Government Departments were chosen from the Eastern Wing) and, in addition, he had instructed the Chief of Staff of the Army to double the recruitment of East Pakistanis forthwith as an earnest of other measures, shortly to be taken, to enhance East Pakistani representation in the Armed Forces.

Throughout the summer and autumn of 1969, the President maintained close touch with political leaders of the numerous parties which had grown up, trying to obtain some measure of agreement on the question of how best power could be transferred to the representatives of the people. Already, in the July address, he had identified three main issues which needed to be resolved: whether West Pakistan should be divided into the original Provinces of which it had been composed; whether adult suffrage throughout the country should take the place of the rather artificial parity between East and West, regardless of differences in population, which had marked the earlier constitutions; and what should be the relationship between the Centre and the Provinces composing the Federation of Pakistan. By November he was able to report that although there were still many differences of opinion between the various parties and individual political leaders over the methods to be used for the transfer of power to the people, there was something like a consensus over the three issues, which would enable him to take them right out of party controversy before the elections were held. Accordingly, West Pakistan would be dissolved into its constituent units; the principle of One man One vote would govern the elections; and both wings of Pakistan should enjoy maximum autonomy consistent with the preservation of the integrity and solidarity of the nation as a whole. Further, he had found a general agreement about a Parliamentary federal form of government, adult franchise, fundamental rights of citizens and their enforcements by the Courts, the independence of the judiciary and its responsibility for preserving the new constitution and the Islamic ideology on which Pakistan was created.

In this same broadcast of November 28, 1969, the President touched upon a number of other important topics. On the exact way in which power was to be transferred, he had not had much help from his consultations; he had therefore decided to take the initiative and prepare a provisional Legal Framework which would enable elections to be held, and the National Assembly brought into being (and later, the Provincial Assemblies) so that a new constitution could be framed. Such a constitution, the President added, would be a sacred document, an agreement for the peoples of Pakistan to live together, so that the voting procedure which the Assembly would decide upon must be fair to the representatives of all regions in Pakistan. This warning from the President, it should be noted in passing, disposes once and for all the allegation that the sweeping victory of the Awami League in the 1970 elections took him by surprise and forced him into a change of plan; it is clear that as early as November 1969, he foresaw the danger lest the representatives of East Pakistan should use their numerical superiority to force the representatives of the other federating units to bow to their will.

The President went on to outline the timetable which he was hoping to follow. He promised the provisional Legal Framework, necessary to enable the elections to be held, by the end of March 1970. The electoral rolls were already being prepared by the Election Commissioners; they would be ready by June 1970, and the constituencies would then be finalized. He fixed the elections for October 5, 1970, and announced that the National Assembly would be required to complete its work of constitution making within 120 days of its first sitting – failing which, the nation would have to be asked to go to the polls again. He expressed the earnest hope that this would not be necessary; and that the Assembly would complete its task so that the constitution which it agreed upon could be authenticated and a national government formed. He also touched upon the problem of dividing legislative and financial powers between the Centre and the federating units; but he saw no reason why the people of East and West Pakistan, bound together as they are by a common historical, cultural and spiritual heritage, should not be able to work out a plan which would satisfy the legitimate desire of the federating units to control their economic resources and development without adversely affecting the vital requirements of the nation as a whole. The President announced that martial law would remain in operation to support this programme for the peaceful transfer of power; but that restrictions on orderly political activity would be withdrawn on the first day of 1970.

That Spring, my wife and I spent some weeks touring Pakistan; two things struck us at once. The first was the intense interest which everyone was showing in political campaigning; the second was the extraordinary pullulation of political parties. It seemed to us as though in West Pakistan almost every man of prominence, almost every section of political and even religious thought, was coming forward with separate programmes. Clearly the underlying theme of most of the programmes was economic; there was a strong feeling that under the last regime, the obviously rising wealth of the country had become concentrated in too few hands. Further, there was a strong tide of hostility to India, especially over Kashmir and over the tragic manifestations of Hindu intolerance of the Muslim minority in certain States. But the political meetings and processions in West Pakistan were on the whole orderly enough, and we came across few examples of organised hooliganism against political opponents. The general mood was very serious. People were asking themselves: 'Where did we go wrong? Are we fated to have a breakdown of law and order and an interregnum of Martial Law every ten years! How can we get ourselves on the right constitutional path again?' And almost everyone we talked to had a slightly different answer to these questions.

In East Pakistan, the atmosphere was not the same. The impression that we formed was that economic problems bulked less largely in shaping the general mood than had been the case during our earlier visits; possibly, we thought, the undoubted progress which the country was making in the material sphere had begun to make some impact. Everyone to whom we talked seemed pleased with President Yahya Khan's recognition that East Pakistan ought to take a larger part in national affairs, and with the tangible evidence that he was determined to rectify matters. But they were convinced that it was up to them to look after their own interests now that adult suffrage and the end of artificial parity between East and West wings at the Centre had been accepted. There was a strong feeling that East Pakistan had in the past been treated as a 'colony', to be exploited by West Pakistan; but when we asked for evidence of this, we could get very little, and we concluded in our own minds that this feeling was emotional rather than rational – but none the less formidable for being so. Unless we were mistaken, there was a kind of 'Now we will get our own back' mood, which we feared did not augur well for harmonious co-operation inside the future National Assembly. But only the aged Mullah Bashani preached complete separation from West Pakistan; and this, we were told, was mainly an attempt to outbid Sheikh Mujibur Rahman's Six Point programme.

But the aspect of the political life of East Pakistan which gave us real cause for concern as lifelong friends of Pakistan was the trend towards political violence on the part of the Awami League and its nominally student supporters. As in West Pakistan, there were numerous political groups; but the Awami League seemed determined that none but themselves should hold public meetings or take out processions. Only a few weeks after our visit, they violently broke up a meeting in Dacca of the Jamaat-i-Islami party – this was on January 18, 1970 – killing one person and injuring more than 500. On January 21, they broke up a meeting of the Pakistan Democratic Party at Narayanganj by organized hooliganism. Next day the office of the Jamaat-i-Islam in Dacca was raided, furniture was smashed and documents burned. The Pakistan Democratic Party was again the victim of attack on February 1, when a public meeting in Dacca was forcibly broken up and several people, including Maulvi Farid Ahmed, leader of the Nizam-i-Islam party, received physical injuries. Nor did the Press escape unscathed if it failed to support the Awami League whole heartedly; on February 28 the offices of two Chittagong papers which opposed certain aspects of the Awami League programme were raided and broken up. Although various aggrieved persons and parties registered formal protests at such tactics, nothing much was done to bring them to an end. The authorities in East Pakistan strictly obeyed the President's pledge of impartiality towards all political parties. Unfortunately the result was to give the Awami League virtually a free hand to crush their political opponents by strong-arm tactics and to establish their own claim to back 'the' party which was standing up for the rights of East Pakistan. As such, we found they enjoyed the support of many responsible citizens, who shrugged off their violent tactics as mere manifestations of youthful, ebullient enthusiasm. My wife and I were unable to accept this point of view; to us, what the Awami League was doing to innocent political opponents was exactly like what Hitler's supporters had done to the aristocratic elements in Germany prior to the rise of Nazism. And there was the further danger, we thought, that in a country like East Pakistan, mob violence is easier to start than to stop, and could quickly culminate in complete anarchy.

The President saw the danger, and in the next of his 'Reports to the Nation' broadcast on March 28, 1970, he pointed out that it was the duty of the leaders of political parties to use their influence to curb indiscipline and law-breaking, and that the Government had the right to expect their co-operation in this all-important matter. The nation, he said, could not afford disorder at that juncture. He also remarked, somewhat ruefully, that when the Government, in response to complaints, took action against law-breakers, there was an immediate outcry, sometimes headed by the complainants themselves, that the troublemakers should be released. He reaffirmed the complete neutrality of the Government towards all parties. He had begun his address by announcing that in the fourth Five-Year Plan to be launched on July 1, 1970, there would be great emphasis on social justice, on the removal of disparities between East and West Pakistan, and accelerated development of the more backward parts of the country. He also announced a comprehensive programme of flood control in the East; the World Bank team which had been studying this matter in East Pakistan had come forward with 20 multipurpose projects costing $800 million, for which foreign assistance was already being mobilized.

After surveying what had been done to improve conditions in the spheres of education, labour relations and agriculture, he announced that the dissolution of the One Unit grouping of West Pakistan would be completed on July 1, 1970, and that the Legal Framework Order, enabling elections to be held would be published on March 30. It would form the basis for the operation of the National Assembly in its work of constitution-making. (It is summarised in Appendix 3 of this book.) This framework, the President went on to explain, represented the best assessment that he had been able to make of the general wishes of the people of Pakistan, and he proceeded to draw attention to some of its features. The total strength of the National Assembly was to be 313, of whom 13 would be women. Seats were to be allocated to provinces on the basis of their population in the 1961 census – the latest figures available. Voting procedure would be settled by the Assembly itself; the President again pleaded that the constitution was essentially an agreement to live together, and that all regions must be reasonably satisfied. This constitution, he added, should embody certain principles; the preservation of Islamic ideology: the preservation of the independence, territorial integrity and national solidarity of Pakistan by means of a federal union, founded on free and periodical elections, the independence of the judiciary, fundamental civic rights, the distribution of legislative, financial and administrative powers between the Federal Government and the Provinces so that the Provinces enjoyed the maximum autonomy consistent with the functions of the Central Government in internal and external affairs necessary to preserve the independence and integrity of Pakistan. Finally, the constitution must provide full opportunities for the people of every region to play their full part in national affairs to achieve which the removal of handicapping disparities, particularly economic disparity, must be achieved within a fixed period.

My wife and I had left Pakistan by the time that the Legal Framework Order was published; but it was clear both from the Press comments and from the speeches of the various political leaders that all parties were ready to accept it as a basis for the elections and as a working outline which the National Assembly could use as a guide. But Press reports from East Pakistan also showed that the pattern of political activity which we had seen was showing little change for the better. For example, it was reported on April 12 that a Muslim League meeting in Dacca had been broken up; thirteen people were injured and the principal speaker was attacked by a hostile mob and had to be rescued by the Police. A fortnight later, it was reported that the office of another group of the Muslim League was attacked and revolver shots were fired. Moreover, Sheikh Mujibur Rahman's speeches and messages seemed to be taking a new turn; he was, it appeared, no longer content to claim for East Pakistan its due share and influence in local and national affairs; he had begun to attack West Pakistan in general, and individual West Pakistanis in particular, as being directly responsible for East Pakistan's economic backwardness by looting her wealth; by transferring her capital, and using the foreign exchange that she had earned to boost industrial develop-ment in the West. The facts that these accusations were patently false; that it was West Pakistan which had supplied the capital for East Pakistan's growing industry, that East Pakistan had for long enjoyed the lion's share of development funds and was no longer the principal earner of foreign exchange, did not make this rabble-rousing misrepresentation any less formidable as a political weapon.

In one passage in his next Report to the Nation, broadcast on July 28, 1970, the President noted some broad changes for the better in the conduct of political campaigns throughout the country as a whole; but he noted also that violence had still not been eliminated, that the divisions between the parties had become sharper, and that the spirit of compromise was absent. He deprecated the strength of purely provincial and local outlooks, and called for toleration and a sense of national unity. He reminded everyone concerned of the need for law and order, stating that the Martial Law authorities had deliberately limited their law-enforcement functions in order to nourish political activity; but that this attitude must not be mistaken for weakness. He was able to report that preparations for the forthcoming elections were well advanced. He gave a further assurance of his Government's determination to preserve complete neutrality towards all political parties and to ensure that so far as possible the elections would be completely fair. Meanwhile, he pointed out, things did not stand still, and he proceeded to summarize what his Government had been doing. The fourth Five Year Plan was giving priority to the removal of disparities; urgent priority was being given to flood control in East Pakistan. He announced that some reliefs and modifications had been made in the Budget to help those whom taxation hit hard; he described the process of dissolving West Pakistan into its pre-1955 units; he outlined the course of the country's foreign relations, particularly those with the U S S R and China, as well as with the Arab and R C D countries – Iran and Turkey. Little progress, unfortunately, had been made in settling differences between Pakistan and India; and he deplored the sufferings of the Muslim community during the recent riots in Maharashtra, but he was hopeful that relations would improve.

Just at the time when all seemed set fair for the election which would bring the National Assembly into being, the forces of nature struck two crippling blows at East Pakistan. In September, heavy flooding displaced millions from their homes and disrupted communications. The President therefore postponed the date of the election until December 7 to give time for things to settle down, and fixed the date of the provincial assembly elections for December 17. Meanwhile, both the East Pakistan Government and the Central Government worked all out to bring relief to the sufferers. Unfortunately this calamity was followed all too soon by one of the worst disasters to occur in modern times; a cyclone of unprecedented severity struck the coastal belt of East Pakistan on November 12. A tidal wave 30 ft high swept over offshore islands and four coastal districts, causing something in the neighbourhood of half a million casualties and enormous damage to property. The afflicted areas were completely isolated because of the destruction of the sea and river craft which constituted their normal means of communication. The civil and military authorities, central and provincial, who at once went into top gear in speeding relief work found their task enormously difficult. The President broadcast to the nation on December 3, 1970, outlining what was being done to bring food, medicine and shelter to the afflicted victims of the disaster and expressing the deep gratitude of the nation for the assistance that was being given from abroad. Even so, the disaster, frightful as it was, affected only 8 National Assembly constituencies and 21 Provincial Assembly constituencies, and the President decided against any further postponement of the elections. He reminded the country how far things had moved since March 1969, when he first announced his intention of restoring democratic government; the elections shortly to be held under the Legal Framework Order were the first phase; next would come the framing of the constitution by the National Assembly; thirdly the transfer of power to the elected representatives; and finally the passing of sovereignty to the Assembly and the termination of Martial Law.

The enormous dimensions of the cyclone disaster struck the imagination of the world, and offers of help poured in from every side; from organizations like the World Bank, which proposed a special reconstruction loan, from the Red Cross, from many Governments and from private individuals. Foreign journalists flocked into Dacca as did representatives of various relief organizations. But in the heated atmosphere of political campaigning, these foreigners, for whom travelling to the afflicted areas was virtually impossible because all available means of communication were monopolized by the official agencies, fell an easy prey to the Awami League's criticisms of the Central and Provincial Governments. The disaster itself became just one more item in Sheikh Mujibur Rahman's hate campaign and the wildest stories were

concocted to demonstrate the alleged heartlessness of the Central
and Provincial military and civil officials. It was alleged that the
authorities refused to allow helicopters to carry relief supplies, and
that the Central Government kept them all in West Pakistan. It
was alleged that the Pakistan Navy and Air Force did little or
nothing to help. It was even alleged that the Defence Forces stole
for their own use supplies of blankets sent from abroad. This last
accusation is absurd on the face of it; no soldier, sailor or airman
found in possession of a blanket other than his official issue would
escape a Court Martial.

In the course of two visits to Pakistan in the Spring and early
Summer of 1971, I made it my business to enquire into such
allegations as these. I found that the Defence Forces deeply
resented them; they had worked day and night and to the very
limit of their endurance, to bring relief. I found plenty of impartial
testimony from foreign relief workers who had succeeded in getting
into the field of operations about the sterling work that the Defence
Forces had been doing; their devotion, I was told was beyond all
praise. The Forces, too, had their own stories to tell. They were
often obliged to bury corpses themselves, because survivors refused
to undertake this work unless they were paid ten rupees for each
burial. They said, grimly, that so many beggars flocked to the
relief areas to profit from international bounty that Dacca, in
particular, was almost denuded of professional mendicants.

In point of fact, the efforts made by the authorities to cope with
the disaster were both prompt and vigorous. Within a few hours of
the end of the cyclone, Army medical teams arrived by helicopter
at some of the worst-hit areas, such as Bhola and Hatiya Islands
and Noakhali District. Detachments of the Corps of Signals fanned
out to set up emergency wireless communications. An Army
Operational Centre at once began work in Dacca to co-ordinate the
activities of the military and the civil authorities. The Pakistan
Navy at once went into action; two ships which happened to be
in the vicinity quickly reached Hatiya, Charsaibani, Sandwip and
Qutubia, bringing relief supplies such as foodstuffs and medicines;
and the Naval authorities in Chittagong worked out a comprehensive plan for landing such supplies where they were most needed.
Many people found floating on rafts and logs were rescued and
brought to safety. The Pakistan Air Force joined in at once; all
available transport aircraft were earmarked for relief work, and

systematic drops of food and clothing were made in East Char, Char Lengatha, Cherfesson, and a dozen other places in the distressed areas. Many places were still under water, which the Army had to cross either by shallow draught craft provided by the Army Engineers or by wading, in order to reach homeless and starving people. The soldiers worked day and night, often thigh-deep in water, mending causeways, repairing culverts, and restoring land-communications. All of them – infantrymen, signallers, engineers, doctors and nursing orderlies – were completely equipped with their own supplies, as is the case with all Regular Forces, and by transporting enormous quantities of material which poured in from many sources they saved hundreds of thousands of lives. In addition to the work of dropping supplies to outlying areas which neither the Army nor the Navy could immediately reach, the Air Force undertook the responsibility of receiving, refuelling, and providing technical assistance to the foreign aircraft which flew into Dacca in increasing numbers, bringing relief supplies. The President and a number of high officials of the Central and Provincial Governments toured the afflicted areas and encouraged those working at relief in their efforts.

The Central Government made a point of seeing that all the requirements of the Provincial Government were promptly met. A special cell of the Economic Co-ordination and External Assistance Division was set up to handle the donations in cash and kind that came from abroad and to ensure that they reached the places in need of them with the minimum of delay. Most of the relief-goods were flown direct to Dacca, as were the goods collected in West Pakistan and those offloaded in Karachi, where the handling facilities are on a large scale. Bulk cargoes like rice, wheat and edible oils reached East Pakistan by sea through the ports of Chittagong and Chalna; but rice seeds were flown in direct so that sowing of the winter crop would not be delayed. Pakistan International Airlines lifted free of charge thousands of kilograms of relief-supplies from Paris, Rome, London, Istanbul, Amsterdam, Frankfurt, Beirut, Kuwait, Damascus, Doha, Tokyo and Manila, as well as 350,000 lbs. of goods from Karachi, Lahore and Rawalpindi – which acted as collecting centres for the donations in kind from West Pakistan. The President set up his own Relief Fund, the detailed contributions to which, both from at home and from abroad, were published in full from time to time. Private donations from abroad were allowed a special bonus of 45%, and everything received was promptly passed on to the East Pakistan Government, which was made solely responsible for the distribution of goods and funds. Extensive relief and rehabilitation works were put in hand to provide employment for those people in the distressed areas who had lost their means of livelihood.

Unfortunately all this good work received little publicity in the outside world; it did not provide as interesting 'copy' for the foreign journalists in Dacca as the wild tales of callousness, robbery, maladministration and brutality which were assiduously circulated by the Awami League and its supporters. Such fabrications were uncritically accepted and cabled abroad. Apparently it did not occur to any of those who listened to them to ask why the supporters – especially the younger and more vigorous supporters – of the Awami League did not themselves organize relief efforts to assist both the Defence Forces and the hundreds of devoted civil officials – themselves East Pakistanis – in the enormous task of coping with the aftermath of the cyclone. Before very long, foreign relief workers were able to visit the distressed areas as communications became restored; their tributes to the work of the Defence Forces remained relatively unnoticed – no doubt they did not provide a sufficiently dramatic 'story'. Some foreign correspondents – their ranks were reinforced by a number who came to Dacca to cover the elections – duly reported the enormous effort which the authorities were making; but their despatches did not offset the bad impression which earlier messages had produced on the outside world.

The sufferings caused by the cyclone were, as has been already mentioned, seized upon by Sheikh Mujibur Rahman and his leading henchmen as another item in the long catalogue of the alleged sufferings of East Pakistan at the hands of the Central Government and of the Western Provinces. The authorities were not only accused of making every possible mistake in the handling of the disaster; they were indicted both for neglecting protective measures – though the orators were conveniently silent about what form these should take – and for standing between East Pakistan and the help which was being so generously provided from abroad by stealing the supplies and embezzling the money. Both before and after the elections, the cyclone disaster was used as a powerful incitement to the campaign of hate against the Central Government and the West which was to produce such frightful sufferings in East Pakistan.

S O U R C E S   *General Elections in Pakistan: an Outline*
Elections in World's Third Largest Democracy
White Paper on the Crisis in East Pakistan
(Government Publications)

The elections which were held throughout Pakistan at the end of 1970 presented some unique features. It is rare for the Administration of a South Asian – or for the matter of that, ot any – country to be so entirely disinterested in the precise nature of the results as was President Yahya Khan and the régime over which he presided. As he had made clear time after time, both in public and in private, his one overmastering wish was to make over power to a democratic Government, freely elected by the people of Pakistan, so that he would be in a position to resume his own proper function – that of Head of the Defence Forces. It is true that in the Field Marshal's time, a Martial Law régime had parted with power in favour of a constitutional form of Government; but President Ayub Khan had by then entered the political arena himself, and was looking forward to playing a continued role in guiding the fortunes of his country. President Yahya Khan had no such desire; he had been called to power, not by any system of election, but by the direction of the outgoing President in order to restore the rule of law and 'bring the country back to sanity'. The sooner he could free himself from the responsibilities which he had never sought, and resume his profession as a soldier, the happier he would be. But he had made it clear from the first that he would not do this until the interests of Pakistan as an Islamic polity on the lines first foreshadowed by Quaid-i-Azam Mohammed Ali Jinnah, could be safely handed over to a civilian Government called to power by the will of the people. It is important to appreciate President Yahya Khan's position in this respect, for it has been made the subject of misrepresentation. He regarded himself as the custodian of the interests of Pakistan as a whole, responsible·for discharging this duty fairly and impartially, until such time as he could make it over to other hands. To accuse him, as certain East Pakistanis have done, of aborting the negotiations which took place in March 1971 by 'failing to come forward with a plan', and nullifying the results of the elections in East Pakistan by supporting party leaders in West Pakistan is wide of the mark. It was not his business to back one side or the other; he had given the best guidance that he could in the Legal Framework Order which all parties, both in East and West, had accepted as the basis for the elections; all he wanted – indeed all that he could do within the limitations which he had set for himself – was to persuade the political leaders to adopt a form of procedure which would be fair to all, so that the deliberations of the National Assembly, when it met, would command the respect of the country as a whole rather than rubber-stamp the ideas of one among several federating units.

Elaborate plans had been made to ensure that the elections would be as fair as possible. From the summer of 1969, the Chief Election Commissioner, Justice Abdus Satta and his two judge-colleagues, one from East Pakistan and one from West Pakistan, had been hard at work preparing electoral rolls, delimiting constituencies, and ensuring that every man and woman in Pakistan over the age of 21 knew his or her voting rights and would be in a position to exercise them. Each of the 24 parties competing for power in West and East Pakistan was given its own symbol – a boat, an umbrella, a tiger, a book, and so forth – so that voters who could not read would be at no disadvantage in making their choice. It was found that there were 56,500,000 qualified electors throughout the country. More than 135,000,000 ballot papers were printed, and polling stations to the number of 16,000 in East Pakistan and 14,000 in West Pakistan were set up. A temporary establishment of 300,000 Polling Offices, 30,000 Presiding Officers, and nearly 2,000 Returning Officers and Assistant Returning Officers was made available. Elaborate precautions were taken to prevent impersonation and falsification of the ballot papers.

Since political parties and individual politicians had been able to carry on a wide range of activities ever since President Yahya Khan came to power in 1969 and had been subject to no restrictions at all save those of orderly behaviour from January 1, 1970, the political life of the country was very active right throughout the year. As has already been mentioned, there were in all some 24 political groups, and since no one quite knew how the electors would cast their votes, almost every one of these groups thought that they might have a chance. The result was that President Yahya Khan's sensible plea that they should try to get together and pool their plans did not succeed. But even before polling took place, the political prophets foresaw that two groups in particular seemed likely to gather a good deal of support. In West Pakistan, the extremely able Mr. Z. A. Bhutto, and in East Pakistan Sheikh Mujibur Rahman were 'tipped' for prominence in any new National Assembly. Both were powerful orators, and took full advantage of the mass-media of radio and television to put forward their programmes. Mr. Bhutto and Sheikh Mujibur Rahman were alike in stressing the need for justice in dispensing the fruits of economic progress more widely, in deprecating the over-concentration of wealth in too few hands, and in advocating the nationalization of basic industries. But in other respects their ideas differed widely. Mr. Bhutto, who had been Foreign Minister in one of Field Marshal Ayub Khan's Cabinets, laid considerable stress upon foreign policy in his speeches. He was highly critical of the U S A, friendly to China, and implacably opposed to India until the grievances of the Kashmiris were removed by the exercise of their right to self-determination. His campaign was entirely orderly and was conducted with great skill. His distribution to schoolchildren of miniature swords – the Sword was the emblem of his Pakistan People's Party – aroused great enthusiasm among the group, whose whole-hearted support, in a number of cases known to the present writer, and no doubt in many others also – actually changed the previously-expressed voting-choice of their elders.

Sheikh Mujibur Rahman's platform was much simpler. Running through all his speeches and pronouncements was his indictment of West Pakistan as the sole author of everything that was wrong with East Pakistan. The Central Government, he thundered, was a mere tool in the hands of West Pakistan exploiters, who had robbed, and were robbing, East Pakistan of her capital, of her economic progress, of her foreign exchange, of her sons' right to jobs in the adiminstrative and Defence Services, and of participation both in the conduct of national and local affairs and in the profitable industries built up in West Pakistan on the fruits of this 'colonial-type' spoliation. He had collected round him a band of able academics, who supplied him with carefully selected facts and figures to support his contentions. Of them, some foreign press observers unkindly remarked that they lacked any administrative experience, sense and real knowledge of the country and would be better employed in the class-rooms which they had so lately left. After the disasters of the floods and the fearful cyclone, Sheikh Mujibur Rahman's denunciations sank to the level of a definite campaign of hate against West Pakistan.

Throughout the earlier months of 1970, he and his leading henchmen had travelled far and wide throughout East Pakistan – West Pakistan he did not bother about – establishing in the popular mind the image that he and the Awami League he headed were the sole real champions of the rights of East Pakistan; and that his Six Points were a charter which would make these rights secure for ever. His hearers believed that if they voted for him, all their economic troubles would be ended; that East Pakistan would become rich and prosperous, and that everyone would have adequate food, shelter and clothing. There were many who did not believe all this, knowing too well that the causes of East Pakistan's poverty were not so easily removed; and they were suspicious of his failure to mention what the region had suffered through long years of exploitation by Hindu interests, based on Calcutta, which had done their utmost to hinder the development of the substructure of Muslim expertise and experience which afforded the sole prospect of economic progress. These critics of the Awami League noticed that no word was spoken about this; that there was no mention, either, of the sufferings of Muslims in India which had lately occurred in Maharashtra and elsewhere. But it was found impossible to voice these views in public; the Awami League supporters broke up the meetings of other parties, and terrorized all potential political rivals. A persistent campaign of intimidation was in full swing by the time that the elections were held.

There is one feature of Sheikh Mujibur Rahman's pre-election pronouncements that should be carefully noted. On no occasion did he demand or even hint at the secession of East Pakistan. One of his main appeals to the many voters who were whole-hearted supporters of the kind of Pakistan which Quaid-i-Azam had founded, was that the Six Points would strengthen Pakistan by bringing the West and East regions to a new understanding of each other and by providing a basis for their more effective co-operation. The Awami League's campaign must have been expensive; the League employed thousands of paid supporters among students and schoolchildren of both sexes; its leaders travelled widely and with retinues. No one quite knew where the funds came from; but it seems clear that the League had many Hindu supporters, for its programme appealed to that community. Did it receive financial support from across the Indian frontier? No one knew, although there was a good deal of speculation. Only one thing seems certain: Sheikh Mujib's campaign of 'full rights for East Pakistan and the Six Points' made an enormous appeal, not only to the East Pakistanis as a whole, but also to those members of the local Police and the locally-stationed military and para-military personnel who were Bengali by race. The result was to make him a popular hero, whom scores of hundreds of simple-minded and enthusiastic people would follow almost anywhere he chose to lead them. Thus the responsibility which fell to his lot, even before the elections, might well have sobered a man of a more thoughtful and statesmanlike outlook. But Sheikh Mujibur Rahman, intoxicated by the enthusiasm of his followers and by the frenzied acclaim of the crowds which gathered to hear him, grew steadily less restrained in his utterances.

In December 1970 Pakistan duly went to the polls; the first task was to elect the National Assembly. In East Pakistan, only 57% of the registered voters cast their ballots, as against 69% in the Punjab, 60% in Sind, 48% in the North-West Frontier Province and 40% in Baluchistan. Of the 57% of the electorate who voted in East Pakistan, the Awami League gained 75%; so that in fact it owed its massive victory which eventually gave it 167 seats in a National Assembly of 313, to only 41% of the East Pakistan electorate. Why 43% of the East Pakistan electors did not vote at all is not clear; one official view is that the Awami League strong-arm men saw that none but their pledged supporters reached the polling stations. That there was much intimidation seems proved. Central Government officers who, in February 1971, had assured me that the elections had been held perfectly freely, and without pressure of any kind, informed me ruefully in July that while the statement held good so far as the Government was concerned, it certainly had not applied to the tactics of the Awami

League in East Pakistan. Particularly in the larger centres of population, they had practised intimidation and pressure of every kind; it was only when order was eventually restored that the victims of this organized terrorism dared to complain. In the country districts, it would seem, pressure was not always so effective; but the opponents of the Awami League were marked men, and became among the first targets of the campaign of murder, looting and arson which raged in March, April and early May of 1971, until the armed forces arrived to stop it. The clean sweep which the Awami League made of its political opponents in the elections for the National Assembly was repeated when polling for the Provincial Assembly took place on December 17. It is true that the Pakistan Democratic Party, containing some of the most respected and experienced men in local politics, secured 2 seats; 2 more seats went to specifically religious groups, and there were 7 independents. But few candidates had any real chance unless they carried the Awami League ticket; those who did so secured 288 seats out of a total of 300. A large proportion of them seem to have been 'new men' whose main qualification for Awami League support was enthusiasm rather than previous experience of political life. Most of them were sincerely devoted to Sheikh Mujibur Rahman, now hailed as the saviour of East Pakistan, whose every word was law.

This pattern of selecting 'new men' was also a characteristic of the elections in the West wing. No political group achieved the overwhelming success which had crowned the Awami League's campaign in East Pakistan; the nearest approach to it was scored by Mr. Bhutto's Pakistan People's Party, which won 88 seats. Three competing and mutually-antagonistic sections of the Muslim League could only muster 18 seats between them; specifically religious groups gained the same number. There were 16 successful independents. This fissiparous tendency was again manifested in the elections for the Provincial Assemblies. In the Punjab, the P P P won 113 seats out of 180; the remainder were divided between no fewer than eight splinter groups, with 28 independents. In Sind, the P P P had a bare majority – 32 seats out of 60; again, the remaining seats fell to splinter groups. In the North-West Frontier Province, the P P P could secure only 3 seats out of 40; the largest group was the Wali Khan section of the National Awami Party with 13 seats, followed closely by the Quayyum section of the

Muslim League, with 10 seats. In Baluchistan, the Wali Khan section of the National Awami Party did best with 8 seats out of 20; splinter groups and independents shared the remainder. A very high proportion of the newly-elected members both of the National and Provincial Assemblies entered politics for the first time; and it was notable that quite unknown candidates, bearing Party endorsements, such as that of the P P P, defeated the 'Old Guard' men who had taken part in politics almost from the time when Pakistan became Pakistan and had looked upon seats in the Legislature as almost personal possessions. It was clear that in the West as in the East wing, the electors were seeking a 'new deal'.

In the new circumstances created by the results of the elections, there was obvious danger of the kind of confrontation between the East and the West wings in the National Assembly, which all patriotic Pakistanis wished to avoid. In East Pakistan, as we have seen, the Awami League and its leader were all-powerful; they commanded also an effective majority in the National Assembly, apart from any support that they might expect to receive from small groups opposed to the P P P. How did they propose to use their newly-acquired power? There were some hopeful signs. Sheikh Mujibur Rahman had won the elections on a platform of which the main plank was maximum provincial autonomy; he had repeatedly declared that this autonomy, by securing a fair deal for East Pakistan, would strengthen, not weaken, the country as a whole. He had also stated that his Six Points were negotiable, at least in certain aspects. It was known that Mr. Bhutto also favoured maximum provincial autonomy, and was ready to discuss the Six Points. Moreover, now that Sheikh Mujibur Rahman had the Prime Ministership of Pakistan, along with control over the Central Government, within his grasp if he chose to take them, was it so certain that his intention of reducing the functions of that Government to the barest minimum – or even beyond it – would remain as strong as ever? Like all other political leaders, he had accepted the Legal Framework as the basis of the elections; and this laid down clearly that the Central Government must enjoy the powers necessary for the preservation of the integrity of Pakistan.

President Yahya Khan had high hopes that agreement between the major parties over the general principles under which the

National Assembly would operate could be achieved; and for this purpose he strongly advised the respective Party leaders to use the interval between the elections and the meeting of the Assembly for preliminary discussions which could result in a working understanding between them. In order to give time for this, he thought it wiser to allow about a couple of months before the session opened. He once again warned everyone concerned of the importance of the task which faced the National Assembly; a constitution, he said, was no mere exercise in party manoeuvering; it was essentially 'an agreement to live together'. In fixing the opening of the National Assembly for March 3, he was steering a middle course which he hoped would strike everyone as fair; for Sheikh Mujibur Rahman was pressing for a very early meeting, while Mr. Bhutto and most of the West wing political leaders thought that more time should be left for preliminary consultations and exchanges of view if the National Assembly was not to find itself stultified by sterile debates on points which ought to have been agreed before it met at all. Mr. Bhutto and other West wing political leaders flew to Dacca to begin talks with the Sheikh. The Awami League leader was not pleased at any delay in summoning the National Assembly; but as he had previously assured the President both that the Six Points to begin talks were negotiable and that the main outlines of the future constitution would be settled in talks between the political parties outside the Assembly, he raised no public objection.

The centre of political interest shifted to Dacca, where the Western Party leaders shortly to be joined by the President in an effort to assist the discussions were meeting Sheikh Mujibur Rahman and his colleagues. In the course of these exchanges, the President acclaimed the Sheikh as the future Prime Minister of Pakistan – a title which the Awami League leader did not disavow. But in the other respects the discussions went badly. The Awami League, flushed by its electoral triumph, was in a thoroughly militant mood. Whether this mood affected the leader, or whether it was inspired by him, remains uncertain. What is on record is that the tone and temper of his public pronouncements completely changed over the Six Points. Instead of repeating that they were negotiable, now that the interests of East Pakistan were adequately protected by the dominant position which the Awami League had won in the National Assembly, he asserted that every one of them must be embodied in the new constitution, and people who did not agree with them could do what they liked about it. Instead of repeating that he stood, not for secession but for regional autonomy, he said that the majority of the population of Pakistan living as they did in 'Bangla Desh' could not 'secede', but that they had the right to autonomy and economic and social freedom. There was no more talk about strengthening Pakistan and preserving its unity.

Sheikh Mujibur Rahman grew more and more adamant over the Six Points; and it became painfully apparent that he had lost interest in anything but the future of East Pakistan. He consistently referred to this Wing as 'Bangla Desh' instead of by its former name. He refused to visit West Pakistan or to meet the President there for further talks, sending General Yahya Khan a message to the effect that if the Six Points were not accepted in their entirety 'rivers of blood will flow'. Meanwhile, the political leaders of the West Wing Provinces who had been elected to the National Assembly became more and more uneasy at the uncompromising attitude of Sheikh Mujibur Rahman; and when the President decided on February 13 to summon the National Assembly to meet at Dacca on March 3, Mr. Bhutto – not without justification, as it would seem to an outside observer – decided that he and his P P P representatives would not attend the National Assembly unless the majority party gave some assurance of their willingness to show reciprocity. He added: 'I think we can work out something which will satisfy both of us. But if we are asked to go to Dacca only to endorse the constitution which has already been prepared by the Awami League and which cannot be altered even an inch here or an inch there, then you will not find us at Dacca'. In reply, Sheikh Mujibur Rahman was uncompromising. On February 21 he said: 'Our stand is absolutely clear. The constitution will be framed on the basis of Six Points.'

In view of these attitudes on the part of the P P P and the Awami League, the President thought that his only course was to allow more time for consideration before the Assembly met. He therefore announced the postponement of the meeting until a later date. In this statement, issued on March 1, he surveyed the history of his successive steps to achieve the peaceful handing over of power to a constitutional government, and, while reiterating his determination to continue on the same course, explained to the nation the difficulties which had arisen because of the absence of give-and-take among the leaders. He had taken the decision to postpone the meeting of the National Assembly, he said, with a heavy heart; but if so many representatives of West Pakistan kept away there was a real risk that the Assembly might disintegrate and all that had been done previously to ensure a smooth transfer of power to it might be wasted. The President gave a solemn assurance that he would summon the Assembly just as soon as constitution-making became a possibility.

Sheikh Mujibur Rahman, flushed with success and secure, as he thought, in the charismatic image with which his supporters had invested him chose to take the view that the President had become the obedient tool of West Pakistan sentiment. The possibility that the President was acting as a true Pakistani, anxious only for the good of the country as a whole, and trying his best to hold an even balance between West and East seems never to have occurred to him. Instead, he decided to see the postponement of the meeting of the National Assembly as a 'conspiracy against "Bangla Desh" '. To foil this conspiracy, he called a general strike, announcing that it was the sacred duty of each and every Bengali in every walk of life, including Government employees, not to cooperate with 'anti-people forces'. In taking this drastic action, it may be that he was encouraged by an incident which seemed well calculated to cause embarrassment to General Yahya Khan by importing external influences into the uneasy internal situation of Pakistan's political life.

On January 30, a Fokker Friendship aircraft of the Indian Airlines Corporation made an unscheduled landing at Lahore Airport. Enquiries revealed that two of the passengers, claiming themselves to be 'Kashmir Freedom Fighters' had hijacked the plane on a routine flight from Srinagar to Delhi and had forcibly diverted it to Lahore. They threatened to blow up the plane along with the crew, the passengers and themselves, as a protest against the externment of Opposition Leaders by the Indian-supported Kashmir Government prior to the Indian General Elections. Feeling against the Indian Government was already strong in the Punjab, and when the hijacking of the plane became known, there was great public enthusiasm. The Pakistan Government were in an awkward situation; under international convention the hijackers should be arrested. But they refused to leave the plane. With great difficulty, they were persuaded to release the passengers and crew, who were taken to the best hotel in Lahore, provided with clothing and other necessities and given full V I P treatment before being taken to the Indian frontier. Several of them later thanked the Pakistan authorities for the care and consideration which had been shown to them. The Indian High Commissioner was informed, was assured of the efforts of the Pakistan Government to return the plane safely, and was invited to send a representative to the spot if he so desired. But in the meantime, the two hijackers were acclaimed as popular heroes; they gave a Press Conference – one of them always remained on the plane – and asked for political asylum. Since the Pakistan Government have consistently refused to acknowledge India's occupation of part of Kashmir, holding that Kashmiris are not Indian nationals, the request was granted.

This action, and the reasons for taking it, hit India on a very sensitive spot; the reaction by Indian Press and public opinion was immediate and bitter. Pakistan was accused of engineering the entire incident. Threats were made to the lives of the Pakistan High Commissioner and his Staff in New Delhi; and there were ugly mob demonstrations against Pakistan. The excitement in India was increased when the two hijackers, in the middle of the efforts of the Pakistan authorities to persuade them to leave the plane so that it could be returned to India, blew it up. The Indian Government announced that it held Pakistan responsible for the blowing up of the plane, neglecting the contention that the hijackers were neither Indian nor Pakistani nationals and thus not a Pakistani responsibility, and demanding compensation for the plane. Without giving the Pakistan Government time to reply, India unilaterally suspended all flights by Pakistani aircraft, civil and military across Indian territory between East and West Pakistan. The Pakistan Government protested strongly at what they regarded as a serious breach of international convention, and declined to give up the two hijackers to a country to which, in their view, the two men did not belong. They offered to settle the incident in a reasonable spirit of compromise. India did not agree; hostile demonstrations against Pakistani nationals persisted, and the ban on over-flying was not lifted. Anti-Muslim riots broke out in Ahmadabad and Baroda, and relations between the two countries became very strained.

Nothing could have suited Sheikh Mujibur Rahman better than

the imposition of this embargo upon the main communication-line between West and East Pakistan at the time when certain of his followers, and possibly himself, were working for a drastic weakening of the power of the Central Government. My wife and I had personal experience of what the ban on over-flying meant to Pakistan. On February 5, 1971, when we happened to be in Karachi, we were invited to accompany Mr. S. U. Durrani, then Managing Director of Pakistan International Airlines, on the first of the long flights right round the southern tip of India and over Ceylon which India's refusal of the normal and long-standing over-flying right necessitated. The journey between Karachi and Dacca, customarily taking less than three hours, was stretched to nearly seven hours, making it one of the longest non-stop flights anywhere in the world. It was well within the capacity of the long-range high-ceiling Boeings which P I A possesses; but the strain upon both cockpit and cabin crews was enormous. This strain, along with the added hours of duty, was most cheerfully accepted; the morale of the Airline was staggeringly high. The same held true of the ground staff and maintenance personnel. We were deeply impressed. At one point in our flight, our aircraft was under supervision by Indian Air Force fighter planes, watchful to see that we did not stray into Indian territorial waters. Yet in spite of all difficulties, Pakistan International Airlines were determined that communications between East and West Pakistan should not be interrupted. And they succeeded. We were informed that plans to deal with such a situation as that which had arisen were already in existence; they were put into operation without delay. There was no need for improvisation on the spur of the moment.

Rather naturally, public opinion in West Pakistan began to speculate whether the hijacking of the plane and the ban on over-flying which followed, so convenient for Sheikh Mujibur Rahman and the Awami League, were as 'spontaneous' as they had been represented. Weight was lent to these rumours by the publication of a letter from Sheikh Abdullah – one of the externed and perhaps the best-known of all the Kashmiri leaders – to the Indian humanist Mr. Jaya Prakash Narayan, published by the *Indian Express* of New Delhi on February 15, 1971. Sheikh Abdullah roundly accused the principal hijacker, Hashim, of being actually an Indian agent, whose plan for seizing the plane and creating an international incident was known to the authorities in Srinagar and New Delhi. In order to ascertain if these statements were correct, President Yahya Khan appointed a judicial enquiry commission, under Mr. Justice Noorul Arfin, of the High Court of Sind and Baluchistan. The enquiry took a considerable time, involving the examination of the hijackers themselves and of a number of witnesses; its report was presented on April 15, 1971. After taking all the available evidence, the commission concluded that the local Pakistan authorities had done everything in their power both to release the crew and passengers of the aircraft and to secure the safety of the aircraft itself in order to return it to India; but that when the hijackers realized that the steps taken to isolate them completely and to take possession of the aircraft were likely to be effective, there was no possible means of preventing them from blowing it up. Of the hijackers themselves, the commission found that Hashim, the principal, was in close contact with, and under the supervision of, Indian Intelligence Agencies, without the cooperation of which he could not have entered the aircraft at all. Moreover, the revolver and the hand grenade carried by the hijackers were later found to be dummies – no doubt to ensure that the lives of the Indian crew and passengers were never in any real danger. The commission concluded that the entire incident had been engineered from the Indian side, with the object of providing a pretext for banning overflights of Indian territory and disrupting communications between the East and the West wings at a time when pourparlers between the Awami League and the Pakistan People's Party were being held in Dacca. (See Appendix No. 4.)

The Indian Press scoffed at the report; but there could be no denial that the whole incident was most useful to Sheikh Mujibur Rahman, who had from the first put all the blame for it on his own Government. To what extent the ban on overflying may have stiffened his attitude may perhaps never be known; but the obstacle thus placed on normal East-West communications must assuredly have strengthened his confidence and his feeling of security in rejecting any kind of compromise with the political leaders of West Pakistan. Doubtless he felt that with East Pakistan, as he thought, virtually isolated, the Central Government would be obliged to accede to his demands. As already noted, he proceeded to show his power by ordering a general strike from the beginning of March.

The declared nature of this strike was peaceful non-co-operation. But as Mr. Gandhi's experience had shown so many times, peaceful non-co-operation requires not only dedicated, unselfish idealism, but also a high degree of discipline and self-restraint. The followers of Sheikh Mujibur Rahman and the Awami League soon showed themselves incapable of conducting themselves on these standards, and serious disorders broke out. The sheer list of these belies the later assertions of the supporters of 'Bangla Desh' that the movement was peaceful and orderly. What happened in Dacca during the first week of March may be cited as illustrating how law and order broke down. Later incidents in Dacca, like those in Chittagong, Jessore, Khulna, Rangpur, Dinajpur, Comilla, Saidpur, Mymensingh, Bogra, Rahshahi, and other outlying centres, are noted in Appendix No. 5.

On March 1, Awami League militants looted and burned many shops and houses and raided the Narayanganj Rifle Club for arms. Almost all the students of Dacca University, except committed militants, had gone to their homes. Iqbal Hall and Jagannath Hall were used as centres from which armed gangs dispersed to collect arms, vehicles and money. On March 2 two firearms shops were looted and the arms taken to an arsenal which was being started in Jagannath Hall. Practice firing in the University grounds was heard all day. On the previous night there had been looting and arson; encouraged by the fact that the troops were confined to barracks on the orders of the Governor, mobs armed with firearms, staves and iron bars raided business premises in Jinnah Avenue and Baitul Mukarram. The Shalimar Hotel and the Gulistan Cinema were attacked and set on fire. Police Officers reported that they could no longer trust their rank and file to deal with the mobs, and asked for the assistance of the military. This was granted, and a curfew was imposed. An Army unit was attacked at Sadrghat and in the firing, six rioters were killed. There was extensive defiance of the curfew, and in spite of the efforts of the military, arson and looting continued throughout the night. On March 3, mob violence spread to other parts of Dacca, particularly Islampur, Patnakhali Bazar, and Nawabpur. Shops, private houses belonging to non-supporters of the Awami League and business premises were looted and set on fire. In the disturbances, five people were killed and 62 wounded. Sheikh Mujibur Rahman announced the launching of a campaign of complete civil disobedience, and ordered the closing of schools and colleges, so that all students, except hard-core militants, who had not yet left for home proceeded to do so. Violent intimidation continued against all who were not active supporters of the Awami

League; radio and T V stations in Dacca were compelled to play the new national anthem of 'Bangla Desh'. More raiding of arms shops and more looting took place. On March 5, telephone and telegraph employees ceased work, and ordinary communications between East Pakistan and the outside world, and between Dacca and other parts of East Pakistan came to an end. On the night of March 5-6, militant students tried to set fire to the British Council premises, but troops arrived in time to drive them off. On March 6 there was a jail-break of 341 prisoners from the Central Prison. During the escape, 7 prisoners were killed when the warders fired; a sergeant and six warders were wounded. The escaped prisoners, joined by Awami Leaguers and activist students, paraded through the streets of Dacca shouting anti-Pakistan slogans. The Government Science Laboratory in Dacca was seized and all available explosive chemicals were taken, but a raid on the Polytechnic was foiled when troops arrived to disperse the mob.

Whenever the troops went into action, a minimum of force was used; they did not interfere with peaceful processions or political meetings, but only with mobs engaged in looting and arson. But the fact is that there were far too few of them to maintain order effectively in an enormous city like Dacca! and with the virtual breakdown of the machinery of civil government because of the campaign of non-co-operation – a campaign rigorously enforced by intimidation of every kind – the situation both in the capital and in many other places throughout East Pakistan became completely chaotic. It was widely believed that nothing could break the hold of Sheikh Mujibur Rahman and the Awami League over the country; and that the Army, scattered as it was in small groups except for larger bodies stationed clear of the Indian frontier, would be helpless in the face of the Awami League's determination to achieve full control. More-over, as was pointed out by responsible foreign correspondents, the Army's Eastern Command consisted of only one division of 15 battalions, of which 9 were from West Pakistan. The remaining six were sections of the East Bengal Regiment, almost exclusively Bengali by race in the rank and file, and also the Commissioned ranks, except for a mere sprinkling of West Pakistanis, mostly in junior positions. There were 3,000 men in the East Bengal Regimental Centre at Chittagong alone; while the East Pakistan Rifles numbered 14,000 fully armed and trained men. In addition, the para-military force of Ansars, who guarded the actual frontier in pursuance of the long-standing policy of keeping the Regulars well back to minimize border clashes numbered about 100,000. Among these bodies of men, as later became clear, Sheikh Mujibur Rahman's propaganda had made great headway; and in addition to their own equipment of mortars, recoilless rifles, heavy and light machine guns, and full transport, there was a steady supply, as later captures proved, of rifles, ammunition and plastic explosives from across the Indian border, the Indian and foreign markings of which spoke for themselves.

Sheikh Mujibur Rahman must thus have felt himself completely secure even if it came to a clash of arms; for with the support of the Police, most of whom were with him, could he not count on something like 176,000 armed Bengalis as against only 10,000 soldiers from West Pakistan? Moreover he was confident that with the ban on over-flying, there could be no reinforcements coming from West Pakistan. Accordingly he seized upon the firing of the Army on the looters and rioters in Dacca to hail those who fell as martyrs; and on March 7 he announced plans for setting up a parallel government of his own. These included the complete closure of all educational institutions, Government Offices and Courts; the stopping of all remittances to West Pakistan; and the organization of Revolutionary Councils in every union, mohalla, thana, sub-division and district who were to take over the administration under the direction of local Awami League units. Later, the original directive to pay no taxes was modified to ensure that taxes were collected, but were to be paid into two private banks. Detailed directives were issued to the Press and to the radio and T V stations ensuring that nothing went out which did not conform to the liking of the Awami League. In the days which followed, the Awami League and their supporters, reinforced by the lawless elements which, in Pakistan as elsewhere, are always ready to take advantage of any disturbance of the peace, ranged unchecked through the streets of Dacca, terrorising possible opponents and molesting the persons and properties of non-Bengalis. Many peaceful citizens, including those in high positions, went in fear of their lives and of the lives of their families; even the Chief Justice did not dare to administer the oath of office to the new Governor, Lt.-General Tikka Khan, until the Awami League's reign of terror had been brought to an end. Nor were these things confined to Dacca; in many places in East Pakistan frightful atrocities were inflicted by Awami

League ruffians upon non-Bengalis and upon all who were not open supporters of Sheikh Mujibur Rahman. There seems to have been little trace of religious intolerance about the killing, beatings and burnings: the criterion was political, and Muslims suffered as much as Hindus. But no doubt the occasion was seized to pay off old scores and gratify private greed and enmity. Particularly serious rioting took place at Chittagong on March 3 and at Khulna on March 5, resulting in hundreds of casualties. As already mentioned, these occurrences are summarized in Appendix No. 5. To add to the growing anarchy, the East Bengal Regiment, the East Pakistan Rifles and the bulk of the para-military frontier security guards, so far from using their strength to restore law and order, manifested their sympathy with the local Awami League leaders.

There was general expectation among the correspondents of foreign newspapers, who had gathered in considerable numbers in Dacca, that Sheikh Mujibur Rahman, who had promised to make an important declaration on March 7, would proclaim 'Bangla Desh' as an independent republic. In fact, he did not do this, although the new flag which had been designed for the purpose flew over his house. He contented himself with talking about the Republic of Bengal, and put forward a series of demands which he no doubt hoped would oblige the Central Government either to lose face by yielding to them, or to take the blame for forcing him into unilateral action. To grasp the implications of the position, it is necessary to turn to the efforts which the President was making to promote conditions in which the National Assembly could be summoned.

S O U R C E S *The President's Broadcasts and Announcements in 1971*
                  Dawn *(Karachi)*, Pakistan Times *(Rawalpindi)*,
                  Pakistan Observer *(Dacca)*, The People *(Dacca)*

It seems likely that President Yahya Khan, like so
many other people both inside and outside Pakistan, found some
difficulty, during February and March 1971 in understanding the
change which had come over Sheikh Mujibur Rahman's public
attitudes after the elections. Granted that East Pakistan had certain
grievances – although to what extent these grievances were the fault
of the Central Government and to what extent they were the sad
legacy of her earlier history was open to question – it could hardly
be denied that for a number of years the Central Government had
been making earnest efforts to deal with them. The specific objective
of raising the living standards of East Pakistan, of securing her full
participation both in the shaping of national policy and in every
branch of the administrative and defence services figured prominently both in the latest Five Year Plan and in the Legal Framework
Order which was to provide a working-paper on which the National
Assembly could begin its discussions directed to the framing of the
new constitution. And how could the legitimate interests of East
Pakistan be promoted more effectively and more rapidly than by
Sheikh Mujibur Rahman himself, with his secure majority both in
the National Assembly and in the Assembly of East Pakistan, pro-
ceeding to form a government under the new constitution and taking
control of national affairs as Prime Minister? This course of action
seemed so obviously expedient, not only for the country in general,
but for East Pakistan in particular, that the Sheikh's apparent intention of refusing it was for some time looked upon as a political
manoeuvre to strengthen his bargaining position. Surely he could
not be so blind to realities as to turn his back upon an opportunity
of such magnitude? Particularly as East Pakistan, like all the other

federating units which were to make up the Republic of Pakistan under the new constitution, was assured of the maximum control of its own affairs, financial as well as administrative, compatible with Pakistan continuing as a country with its own international personality?

There is conclusive evidence that although President Yahya Khan, in his broadcast of March 1, 1971 had reluctantly decided to postpone summoning the National Assembly until there was enough basic understanding between the various political parties to minimize the risk that it might break up infructuously, he still hoped that cool and rational discussion might lay the necessary foundations for a meeting. As the parties seemed deadlocked, he decided that he would try himself to bring them together. Accordingly on March 3, he invited twelve of the elected members of the National Assembly, representing the leaders of all political parties, to meet him in Dacca for a conference on March 10. He added that he saw no reason why the Assembly should not meet within a couple of weeks of the conference. To his great disappointment, Sheikh Mujibur Rahman and the Awami League refused to attend, so that this new *démarche* failed before it had begun. In face of this refusal, no representatives of East Pakistan dared to accept the President's invitation.

Undaunted by this setback, General Yahya Khan tried again. In a nationwide broadcast on March 6, he outlined what he had been doing to bring the parties together and why he had postponed the meeting of the National Assembly. He thought, he said, that this postponement would save the Assembly and all the effort that had gone into the making of it; and would at the same time allow passions to cool and fruitful discussions to take place. But the postponement had been misrepresented, whether deliberately or otherwise he could not say; and had been made the occasion for serious outbreaks of disorder, of the kind that no Government could tolerate. But in order to avoid adding to the tension, he had specifically ordered the authorities in East Pakistan to use the very minimum of force in stopping law-breakers from loot, arson and murder. Further, since his efforts to reach agreement among the various political leaders about the date for opening the National Assembly had failed, he had decided to fix it himself for March 25. The President added a stern warning that he owed a duty to millions of people in East and West Pakistan to preserve the integrity of the country; and that so long as he remained in control of the Armed Forces, whose duty it is to ensure the integrity, solidarity and security of Pakistan – a task, he added, in which they had never failed – he would discharge this responsibility faithfully.

So far from heeding this warning, Sheikh Mujibur Rahman's response to the President's address was to lay down four conditions which, he said, must be satisfied before he and his party would even consider attending the National Assembly on March 25. These four points were: immediate withdrawal of Martial Law; immediate withdrawal of all military personnel into barracks; an enquiry into the casualties inflicted by the shooting; and immediate transfer of power to the elected representatives of the people prior to the meeting of the National Assembly. Meanwhile, the confusion and terror resulting from his 'parallel government' and the atrocities committed by his Awami League hooligans spread widely through East Pakistan. The President's orders about the use of minimum force were so strictly obeyed that the Sheikh and his followers evidently considered that the Army was powerless. The second of his four-point demand had long been complied with in the sense that the military had never attempted to occupy Dacca and other cities: they only emerged from their barracks when a particularly serious outbreak of arson and looting had to be checked; for the rest of the time they were not seen in the streets at all. In the light of later events, many people have wondered if this policy was not mistaken, and if some more tangible evidence of a 'military presence' might not have saved trouble. But the President was determined that his efforts to arrange a meeting of the National Assembly should not be hampered by giving Sheikh Mujibur Rahman any pretext to claim that political negotiations were being conducted under the threat of force. As it turned out, the Awami League leader had no such delicacy of feeling as he was credited with; he seized upon the carefully-limited action of the armed forces to make resounding declarations that seventy million Bengalis would not hesitate to make the supreme sacrifice to win the status of free citizens in a free country, calling upon them to turn every house into a fortress.

President Yahya Khan made a supreme effort to solve the impasse caused by Sheikh Mujibur Rahman's 'take it or leave it' attitude. Since the Sheikh would not come to see him, he went to Dacca on March 15 to see the Sheikh.

There followed some ten days of complicated discussions, in which the President plainly showed himself sincerely anxious to prevent a breach between the Eastern and Western political leaders. On March 17 his advisers met an Awami League team and drafted a regulation to set up a Council of Ministers drawn from the elected members to advise the Governor of each Province, and to arrange that Martial Law would recede gradually into the background. Further, the third of the Sheikh's four points was met by the offer of a commission to enquire into the circumstances in which the Army acted in aid of the civil power. This was to be headed by a Judge of the High Court of East Pakistan to be selected by the Chief Justice; its members were to consist of men drawn from the Civil Service, the Police, the Army and the East Pakistan Rifles. Next day, March 18, Sheikh Mujibur Rahman rejected the Commission on the grounds that the appointment would be made under a Martial Law Order and that the report would be made to the Martial Law authorities. In view of the fact that the country had been under Martial Law since 1969, this objection would appear to lack substance, and seems to be further evidence of Sheikh Mujibur Rahman's reluctance to co-operate. His next step, on March 19, was to insist to the President that the draft Martial Law regulation framed on March 17 should provide for investing the National and Provincial Assemblies with legislative powers accompanied by representative government in both spheres, and that there should be complete withdrawal of Martial Law.

There were obvious legal difficulties in such a plan. If the proclamation of Martial Law on March 25, 1969 was revoked, what validity would attach to the instrument establishing the Central and Provincial Governments? The Awami League representatives urged that these were really political, not legal, issues, and should be resolved in a political manner. The President felt uneasy; but agreed that his advisers should draft another Martial Law regulation in an endeavour to meet the Awami League's wishes. This draft regulation provided for the setting up of Central and Provincial Cabinets, for investing the National and Provincial Assemblies with the powers that they enjoyed under the dormant 1962 Constitution; the abolishing of Martial Law administrators and military Courts, but retaining for the time the Presidential function of Chief Martial Law Administrator to avoid the risk of a legal vacuum. The President was hopeful that progress was being made, and asked three West Pakistan leaders representing the Council Muslim League and the Jamiat-e-Ulema-e Islam to meet him in Dacca. The fact that a very serious provocation by the Awami League rowdies took place in Chittagong and Joudevpur, where the normal unloading of Army supplies from a ship was obstructed in one case and a convoy was attacked in the other, did not interrupt the negotiations, although it was proof, if further proof were needed, of the contemptuous attitude which Sheikh Mujibur Rahman's followers were adopting both to the Army itself and to all constituted authority.

When the President next met Sheikh Mujibur Rahman and his principal lieutenants on March 20, he made it clear that his agreement to whatever plan was settled on for the handing over of power depended upon its acceptance by all political leaders. He further stated that the legal validity of the proposed proclamation would have to be examined by experts. The President's advisers were doubtful about this point, but the Awami League representatives promised to produce their own legal expert, Mr. A. K. Brohi, in support of their views. This fundamental question was for the moment set aside; and a set of objectives was drawn up for examination by both sides. The first was for lifting Martial Law; the second was the setting up of Central and Provincial Cabinets; the third, the investing of Central and Provincial Assemblies with legislative powers; the fourth that East Pakistan, in view of its geographical situation, should enjoy a greater degree of provincial autonomy than other Provinces; the fifth, that further discussions should take place about the exact way in which all these objectives could be reached. It was pointed out to Sheikh Mujibur Rahman that until the National Assembly, to be summoned on March 25, ratified the proclamation for achieving them, Martial Law ought to continue. He did not agree. But in order not to hold matters up, a number of salient points which the proposed proclamation would have to cover were drawn up. (Appendix No. 6.) But on March 21, an ominous note was introduced into the discussions; in an unscheduled meeting with the President, Sheikh Mujibur Rahman stated that he no longer wanted the setting up of a Central Cabinet. At this juncture, Mr. Z. A. Bhutto reached Dacca at the President's invitation, and in spite of Sheikh Mujibur Rahman's publicly announced refusal to meet the P P P leader, the President persuaded the two men to hold a joint meeting with him on March 22. At this meeting, according to the official record, another unexpected development occurred; Sheikh Mujibur Rahman requested the withdrawal of the Presidential Order summoning the National Assembly on March 25. He refused a suggestion that it should be summoned on April 2 to give legal cover to the proposed proclamation. It seemed an appropriate sequel to his attitude that on that same evening the Central Students' Action Committee should announce that March 23, customarily celebrated as Pakistan Day throughout the country, would in East Pakistan be observed as 'Resistance Day'.

The amended draft proclamation had been handed over to Mr. Bhutto of the P P P and to Mr. Tajuddin Ahmed of the Awami League for discussion. The P P P held that after Martial Law was lifted and before it was ratified by the National Assembly, the proposed proclamation would have no legal sanction; they suggested that it should either be endorsed by the National Assembly or, if published, should not take effect until after such endorsement. As an alternative, they thought, the President might continue as Chief Martial Law Administrator to provide the legal cover until the National Assembly so acted. They further suggested that a clause should be added providing that no law or constitution could be presented to the National Assembly unless it was approved by a majority of the members of each Wing. They were also anxious to know if the Legal Framework Order would be protected.

Although on March 23 there were armed rallies and demonstrations and the 'Bangla Desh' flag was hoisted, the constitutional discussions continued. The Awami League refused to work on the draft proclamation which until then had been the working-paper, and produced one of their own. In this new draft, which did not seem to take account of the legal difficulties already under discussion, several novel proposals were put forward. Among them were: members of the National Assembly elected 'from the State of Bangla Desh' and the states of West Pakistan were to be sworn and set up separately to frame constitutions for the 'State of Bangla Desh' and for the states of West Pakistan; there was an alteration in the Oath of Office laid down in the Legal Framework Order; more revealing still was the suggestion that the National Assembly should proceed to frame a constitution for the 'Confederation of Pakistan' – an expression applicable only to an agreement between independent sovereign states to join together for certain purposes. This, along with other provisions which would have left the Central Government a mere ghost, without taxation-powers to raise funds even for the shadowy functions allowed to it, ran clean contrary both to the Legal Framework Order and even to Sheikh Mujibur Rahman's own Six

Points – one of which provided that Pakistan shall be a Federal Republic. The serious implications of a proclamation of this kind, which was intended to serve the purpose of an interim constitution, were pointed out both by the President's own advisers and by the representatives of West Wing political parties; but the Awami League representatives refused to modify one single point. Mr. Tajuddin Ahmed indeed went so far as to say that even this proclamation would be too late if it did not issue within the ensuing 48 hours. It was in vain that a number of distinguished political leaders called upon Sheikh Mujibur Rahman in the hope that he would adopt an attitude which would leave room for the views of other people. They found him completely inflexible, elevated in spirit by a vast procession of armed volunteers parading past his house. It was on the evening of March 24 that the President had his last meeting with the Awami League leaders. They declined to alter their stand as set out in their own draft proclamation; and in a subsequent news conference Mr. Tajuddin Ahmed announced: 'From our side there is no need of further meetings.' In other words, their proclamation was their ultimatum.

It is important to get this point clear; for 'Bangla Desh' supporters have subsequently attempted to argue that the talks were arbitrarily terminated by the President and his advisers on a mere legal point which could have been got over. This is casuistry; the legal point, important as it is, was not the breaking-point; with give and take on both sides, a way round it could perhaps have been found. What in fact made further discussion fruitless – not that the President broke off talks even on this – was the Awami League ultimatum as embodied in their draft proclamation, and their own statement that from their side there was no need of further meetings. To contend that they left the President, thinking that all was settled and believing that all their demands were 'in the bag' is to falsify the record. They must have known quite well that the draft proclamation, if put into execution, would have extinguished the Government of Pakistan, given *de jure* recognition to the *de facto* parallel administration which they had been attempting to run in East Pakistan since the beginning of March, and created a constitutional vacuum. They must have known, in view of the President's repeated warnings, that his sense of the responsibility which he owed to the country would never allow him to agree to a plan of this kind. The only possible conclusion to be drawn from their behaviour is that they cared nothing for his warnings and were confident that they could set up a 'State of Bangla Desh' regardless of anything that could be done to stop them. And that, as the President later remarked, would have been the end of Pakistan as created by the Father of the Nation. If Sheikh Mujibur Rahman and the Awami League had been even a little less confident in the supposed impregnability of their own position, agreement might still have been possible. But all available evidence shows that their plans were already made to take everything that they wanted by sheer force, unless it was surrendered to them meanwhile. No doubt that was why, on March 23, Mr. Tajuddin Ahmed had stated that unless the Awami League's own proclamation was issued within 48 hours, it would be too late.

While these political negotiations were going on in Dacca, the situation both in the capital and in the outlying cities and districts of East Pakistan was deteriorating rapidly because of the Awami League's persistent defiance of lawful authority and determination to establish its own system of government. Supporters of 'Bangla Desh' are now claiming that Sheikh Mujibur Rahman's followers maintained perfect order – better order than was customary under the legitimate administration. The record does not support this claim; on the contrary, the most terrible excesses of mob violence took place in Chittagong, Khulna, Jessore, Rangpur, Dinajpur, Comilla, Saidpur (where the mob was bold enough to fire upon troops in the cantonment), Bogra, Mymensingh and other places. Under President Yahya Khan's direct orders, the Army was only permitted to intervene in extreme circumstances; for example, it is known that in the serious rioting by large mobs in the first week of March, only 23 people were killed and 26 wounded by Army firing while the total casualties amounted to 172 killed and 358 injured. This policy of restraint allowed the Awami League to take over the machinery of administration virtually unchallenged, and to direct mob violence against its antagonists in an almost scientific manner. Moreover, the League came to believe that it was all-powerful, that nothing could disturb its grip upon the Province, and that it could act as it pleased, without any risk of its actions being challenged by any other authority – still less, that those who perpetuated excesses under its orders might later be brought to book. The mood of Sheikh Mujibur Rahman's supporters may be gathered not only from the speeches of their leaders, but also from the mass of inflammatory printed and cyclostyled leaflets and pamphlets distributed widely throughout the towns and the countryside. These announced that the National Liberation Movement was in progress and incited the people to take up arms, liquidate the 'enemy troops', arm themselves with any weapon that they could find, destroy roads and bridges, and keep bombs and Molotoff cocktails in every house. If attacked, a bloody resistance was to be offered, and an armed struggle of long duration was to be prepared for. In the light of such incitements to violence, it would have been a miracle if all persons who were not known adherents of the Awami League went in fear of their lives and of the lives of their families. All too frequently, as may be seen from the incidents listed in Appendix No. 5, these fears were justified. It is no wonder that in the later days of March 1971, many people fled across the Indian border to escape the prevailing anarchy and violence, and that, in consequence, a serious refugee problem began to emerge.

In some quarters, President Yahya Khan has been blamed for allowing matters to deteriorate so badly as they did in March, 1971. But it is not difficult to understand his very cautious policy. Right until the end of that month, he had believed that the aim, which he had pursued steadily ever since March 1969, when he was called to power, of handing over the control of national affairs to a democratically-elected government, was on the point of fulfilment. The only obstacle, as it seemed to him, which still remained to be overcome, was the uncompromising attitude of certain political leaders whose broad acceptance of common constitutional principles was a prior condition to the effective functioning of the already-elected National Assembly. He hoped up to the very last moment that these uncompromising frames of mind would yield to rational discussion. To picture the President, as supporters of 'Bangla Desh' – including, very unfortunately, the correspondents of certain influential foreign newspapers – now do as a mere puppet in the hands of Mr. Bhutto and other political leaders of West Pakistan, or, more ridiculous still, as being swayed by the views of his own military subordinates against his better judgment, is to ignore the entire course of his policy since March 1969. He regarded himself then, as he still does, as the custodian of the interests of the nation, as independent of every political party in preserving those interests and as bound to hold an even hand between competing claims. With his usual frankness, he admitted, in his address to the nation on March 26: 'I should have taken action against Sheikh Mujibur Rahman and his collaborators weeks ago but I had to try my utmost to handle the situation in such a manner as not to jeopardize my plan of peaceful transfer of power. In my keenness to achieve this aim, I kept on tolerating one illegal act after another, and at the same time I explored every possible avenue for arriving at some reasonable solution.'

On March 24 and 25, circumstances were combining to make the President's policy of cautious restraint in face of intense provocation more and more difficult. On March 24, while the cyclostyled and printed incitements to violence were circulating, serious arson occurred at Golahat, North Saidpur. Moreover, a mob armed with lathis and lethal weapons, numbering some 8,000, converged on Saidpur to attack non-Bengali residents, and fifty homes were set on fire. Next day, the violence continued, Golahat was attacked. Saidpur cantonment was attacked and the troops were fired on. In Chittagong, important not only as East Pakistan's main deep-water port, but as the Headquarters of the East Bengal Regiment, systematic efforts were made to block communications between the port itself and the city. Huge barricades were set up to prevent supplies reaching the cantonment, where some West Pakistani troops were stationed. In Dacca itself, barricades sprang up in many parts of the city; and, as later became clear, Igbal and Jagannath Halls of Dacca University were put in state of defence.

In light of the evidence which later became available, it seems impossible to doubt that a systematic armed uprising was planned shortly to take place. Sheikh Mujibur Rahman had begun to make military appointments. A certain ex-Colonel Usmani was named as Commander-in-Chief of the Revolutionary Forces responsible directly to the Sheikh; while Major-General (Retd.) Majeed and Lt. Commander (Retd.) Moazzam were deputed to enlist ex-servicemen, of whom lists had been prepared in the Awami League headquarters. Arms seem to have presented little difficulty; in addition to those which were coming in substantial quantities across the Indian border, stocks had been piled up by looting arms shops. The Awami League knew also that it could rely upon the bulk of the East Bengal Regiment, the East Pakistan Rifles, and many of the Border Guards, all of whom had their own armaments. So far as Dacca itself was concerned, there would be little difficulty in obtaining the 15,000 rifles and ammunition kept at Police Headquarters. Further, the East Pakistan Rifles and the East Bengal Regiment had their service-type wireless transmitters, so that instructions could be passed quickly. In contrast, perhaps, to the expectations of the rank-and-file of 'Bangla Desh' partisans, who had been warned to prepare for a long-drawn out guerilla-type struggle, it looks very much to the outside observer as though the High Command of the Awami League was banking upon a quick takeover, which would confront the Pakistan Government and the outside world with the *fait accompli* of a 'Bangla Desh', independent, complete with its own Government and its own armed forces, capable of dealing with any internal resistance or with any attack from the outside.

Leaving aside the rhetorical boasts that it was impossible to subdue '70 million Bengalis' by force intended both to encourage supporters and to provide material for foreign journalists converted to the cause of 'Bangla Desh' by arguments that a popularly-elected democratic party was challenging a brutal 'colonial-type exploitation' imposed by a military dictatorship resting on West Pakistan, it is interesting to analyse what grounds Sheikh Mujibur Rahman and his supporters had for assuming that their position was invulnerable. First, no doubt, was the immense numerical superiority in men and armaments, to which attention has already been drawn, between the Bengali forces upon which the Awami League felt that it could rely, and the comparative handful of West Pakistani soldiers. Along with this went complete confidence in massive Indian support, based upon the obvious friendliness of Indian Press comments both upon the Awami League's electoral victory and upon the 'heroic resistance movement' headed by Sheikh Mujibur Rahman. Already there had been a steady trickle of arms from India into the hands of the League's supporters; regular channels of communication had been established across the frontier. It was known that instructors from the Indian armed forces were standing ready to impart their skills to Bengali partisans. Quite as vital to the anticipated success of the Awami League was India's helpful ban upon overflying Indian territory, which, almost everyone believed, would effectively prevent the reinforcement from West Pakistan of the Regular battalions stationed in the East. There was complete confidence on this point – a confidence based upon sheer ignorance of the logistical skill of a highly-trained Army and an extremely efficient airline. Moreover, as a direct consequence of the mistaken theory that East Pakistan had been economically exploited by the Central Government acting in the interest of the West wing, there was a highly exaggerated estimate of the importance of East Pakistan's trade in jute to the entire national economy of Pakistan. In spite of the fact, easily ascertainable from statistics, that for a good many years West Pakistan, not East Pakistan, had earned the bulk of the country's foreign exchange because of its diversified economy and business 'drive', the Awami League leaders held firmly to the erroneous belief that if the foreign exchange earnings of the jute industry were diverted to 'Bangla Desh', the Central Government would be so hard pressed financially that it would be unable to 'afford' to support its troops in East Pakistan. This belief had become a cardinal point in the creed of the Awami League. Unfortunately for Sheikh Mujibur Rahman's plans it was, like so much else in his carefully-contrived campaign of propaganda, based upon a fallacy.

In spite of the enormous damage that the Awami League has inflicted both upon East Pakistan and upon Pakistan as a whole, there is something almost pathetic in the dream world, entirely divorced from hard realities, which it had created for itself and in which it lived, moved, and had its being. The truth is, as that most candid of Indian men of letters, Mr. Nirad C. Chaudhuri wrote a few weeks later in a series of articles published in the *Hindustan Standard* of Calcutta, the people of East Pakistan, along with their leaders, had not for centuries known what formal military operations really entailed. Sheikh Mujibur Rahman and his League plainly thought that they would be able to contain, if not to liquidate, highly-trained professional troops inspired by the courage, *esprit de corps*, and discipline derived from a hereditary tradition of military service. The ruin which they brought upon themselves and upon so many others is a fearful illustration of the permanent validity of Nicolo Machiavelli's grim conclusion that men who confuse what is with what they think ought to be, quickly compass their own destruction. And unfortunately, the 'destruction' was not confined to the prime authors.

No information has so far been published about the precise moment when the plans for a *coup d'etat* based on armed violence came to the notice of the authorities; but it is evident that right up to the last moment, President Yahya Khan was hoping to arrive at an understanding with the Awami League which would stop the rising before it began. In this he failed, not through any fault of his own; and on March 26, in a nation-wide broadcast which echoed his own deep disappointment, he gave an account of his efforts to transfer power by peaceful means, and of the reasons why these efforts came to nothing. He assured the nation that his firm intention of transferring 26 powers to constitutionally-chosen Governments, Central and Provincial, remained unaltered; but that in view of the very grave situation that had developed – and, as mentioned on a previous page, he explained how it happened that he had not dealt with it earlier – he had called upon the armed forces to restore order; he had banned political activity and banned the Awami League as a political party, and had imposed Press censorship.

In this address, the President gave no details of the plans for the armed rising which as became later apparent, his action had nipped in the bud. But it is certainly significant that the first information that the public was given about these details came from of all places – New Delhi. In a message dated March 31, the correspondent of the Columbia Broadcasting Corporation, Mr. Weatherall, reported: 'All the indications are that Mujib and his outlawed Awami League had a carefully advance-planned military campaign. The first target of this "liberation" army was to be Chittagong, East Pakistan's only deep water port. Once the port was destroyed, President Yahya Khan would have difficulty in supplying his troops in East Pakistan. The next stage was the capture of Dacca and to prevent its use as the main base for Pakistan Army operations. It is believed that Mujib had received supplies from outside sources for a long period and that these were hidden till the crunch came from Yahya (on March 26, 1971). Many Western diplomats in New Delhi feel these weapons could only have come from India'.

That this message was broadly correct is apparent from the further details given in the Government of Pakistan's *White Paper on the Crisis in East Pakistan* published on August 5, 1971. In that document, the operational stages are set out as follows. On a signal, to be given in the early hours of Friday morning, March 26, from Awami League Headquarters in Dacca, the following action would be taken: first East Bengal Regiment troops would occupy Dacca and Chittagong to prevent the landing of the Pakistan Army by air or sea; secondly the remaining East Bengal Regiment troops, with the help of the East Pakistan Rifles, Police and armed Razakars (frontier guards) would move to eliminate the Armed Forces at various cantonments and stations; thirdly, the East Pakistan Rifles would occupy all the key posts on the border and would keep them open for aid from the outside. So much for the internal aspect of the plan. But there was an external aspect also. Further requirements of arms and ammunition would be met from India; and Indian troops would come to the aid of the Awami League forces as soon as the first objective of occupying key-centres and paralysing the Pakistan Army had been achieved. It should be noted in passing that because efforts to attain the first objective were so completely frustrated by the Pakistan Army, the second part of the 'external' programme never materialized except in limited, covert and clandestine activity. No considerable body of Indian troops, operating as a unit, faced the Pakistan Army in support of the rebels. This support was confined to small groups, many of whom were captured, whose objective was sabotage and disruption of communications rather than open warfare. Even so, India's undisguised friendship and help to the rebels, and her interference in the affairs of a neighbour -- intereference which violated all the canons of international propriety - greatly hampered the restoration of ordered administration throughout East Pakistan.

Immediately prior to his call upon the Army to take action against the planned rebellion fixed for the small hours of March 26, President Yahya Khan ordered the expulsion of foreign journalists from East Pakistan. Many of them had been in Dacca for some time, covering first the cyclone, and then the activities of the Awami League. They had been carefully cultivated by Sheikh Mujibur Rahman and his followers; some had become enthusiastic supporters of 'Bangla Desh' whose emergence as an independent State they were hourly expecting. This latter group had already succeeded in conveying to the outside world an unfavourable impression of President Yahya Khan and the Central Government, representing both as hostile to the legitimate aspirations of East Pakistan. Others, again, had sent despatches which were both balanced and factual and inspired by high standards of professional impartiality. The President's decision to expel them all, though taken, as he himself has stated more than once, because he felt that he could no longer guarantee their personal safety in the highly-charged atmosphere of Dacca, turned out unfortunately. The Army authorities, no doubt under extreme pressure, were more anxious to get the correspondents safely out of East Pakistan than to consider either their personal convenience or their professional *amour propre*. Many of them deeply resented what they regarded as their cavalier treatment and at least one was heard to remark that he would take the first opportunity of 'getting his own back'. Since many of them went to India, and proceeded to report the events in Pakistan, in a spirit of hostility to the Government and of friendship to the rebel cause, the threat proved no idle one, and did immense damage to Pakistan. The Army was held up to the obloquy of the world as the brutal suppressor of a popularly based movement for freedom and democracy; the wildest and most groundless rumours were reported as unquestioned facts; worst of all, perhaps, wholly imaginary triumphs of the 'liberation army', sheer invention though they were, contributed to the prolongation of what was from the first a hopeless struggle of amateur as against professional forces.

In Dacca, the headquarters of the rebellion, fighting was soon over. Attempts had been made to isolate the forces in the cantonment from the City by the erection of numerous barricades. No fewer than fifty barricades had been erected between the International Hotel in the centre of the residential quarter and Dacca airport. These barricades presented few difficulties to highly-trained troops, whose main object was to remove them with minimum loss of life. Accurate fire soon drove off those who manned them; and snipers' nests in surrounding huts were cleared by the use of tracer bullets which set fire to inflammable materials and obliged the occupants to escape to safety. The main streets were quickly cleared. The only serious resistance which the Army encountered was from the well-armed men of the East Bengal Regiment and the Police, who manned a number of strong-points. These were systematically reduced. The Army never opened fire until it was first fired upon; when this happened, it reacted sharply. In operations of this kind, as recent British experience in Northern Ireland again illustrates, some civilian casualties are inevitable as innocent people are caught in cross-fire; but the Army never fired upon civilians as such, only upon those who resisted it with arms. Many people of the middle and upper class families had already left the city to escape the tyranny of the Awami League hooligans; College and University students had 'gone down', partly because of the approaching Vacation, and partly because of the closure of educational institutions by Sheikh Mujibur Rahman's decree. Jagannath Hall of Dacca University had been turned into an arsenal and strong-point, manned by members of the Students' branch of the Awami League. When troops approached it, they were received with heavy mortar and small-arms fire, which was returned, as a result of which some of the militant students and one or two members of the Staff who happened to be in the building became casualties. One such member, who unfortunately died of his injuries, later admitted that it was his misfortune that he had been there at all; he had entered the building and had not been allowed by the 'garrison' to leave. But all the other two dozen or so Halls of Residence along with the magnificent buildings of Dacca University itself, remained completely undamaged, as my wife and I saw for ourselves when we visited the University in early July. Moreover, there were no signs of any recent patching or repairs. In the course of our visit to Dacca we found that some buildings in the city were damaged, and some shops were still closed; but in our estimation, the capital had already returned to at least ninety per cent of its normal bustling and crowded business activity.

Sheikh Mujibur Rahman was arrested at 1.30 a.m. on the morning of March 26, but a number of his lieutenants, either more wary or less confident than he, fled from Dacca to those parts of East Pakistan which were under Awami League control. They set on foot the most extraordinary stories. It was said that most of Dacca had been razed to the ground; that the Army had mown down peaceful citizens with tanks; that a systematic campaign had been conducted to liquidate the whole intelligentsia of Dacca – writers, artists, professors, University students – the lot. All these stories found their way to the news editors of All India Radio, and were then broadcast, not only to India, but to the world outside. Some at least of these monstrous fabrications were picked up by the British Broadcasting Corporation, and were thus given even wider currency. In some known instances, an All India Radio bulletin, picked up by the B B C, was later given a spurious authenticity by being ascribed to the B B C itself, and was again issued to Indian listeners. Most regrettably, as it turned out, these false rumours were not authoritatively contradicted until a later date, by which time they had been accepted by many countries of the Western World as entirely authentic. Worse still, they were swallowed *in toto* by many members of the East Pakistan community in Britain. Aroused to a frenzy of agitation by anxiety over the fate of their relatives, by fears for their property in Dacca and elsewhere, and by the conviction that the Martial Law authorities were flouting the results of the elections which had called Sheikh Mujibur Rahman to power, they campaigned to enlist the sympathy of many people prominent in political life, including some of those who had, some years previously, advocated the secessionist cause of Biafra on similarly sentimental and unrealistic grounds. The cause of 'Bangla Desh' thus commanded many advocates, and enjoyed considerable financial support.

Some of this support came from the charitable instincts of well-wishers; but a great deal more derived from the astute policy of the Awami League when it was virtually in control of the civil administration of East Pakistan. With a shrewd eye to the needs of the future the League's leaders had arranged to move the cash reserves of the State Bank and of the Dacca Treasury to places from which these reserves could be quickly transferred across the Indian frontier, where they could be used to buy arms and purchase support in India and elsewhere. So great were the losses from this source that the Government of Pakistan was obliged, at great inconvenience, to 'demoneytize' the Five Hundred and the Hundred Rupee notes. But before this was done, substantial funds had been transferred abroad by the Awami League to help the cause of 'Bangla Desh' – a cause which, as will be apparent on a later page, was also supported by the formidable resources and trained skills of India's international public relations network. By the time that the truth about Dacca became known abroad, supporters of 'Bangla Desh' were no longer receptive to it. Even the signed statement of more than fifty professors, artists, newspaper editors, poets and other intellectuals, to the effect that they were quite well, thank you, and that the circulated reports of their death had been much exaggerated (as Mark Twain once remarked in similar circumstances) fell on deaf ears. No: Dacca had been destroyed, its intellectuals massacred, the Army had slaughtered innocent civilians in thousands – and no one was going to persuade them otherwise. They were confirmed in their attitude by the stream of lying reports about the 'freedom fighters'' successes when confronted by the Pakistan Army.

Communications between Dacca and the rest of East Pakistan had been so badly interrupted because of the Awami League's usurpation of civil government during the early weeks of March that, as my wife and I were told by Lt.-General Tikka Khan (who had been duly sworn in as Governor by the Chief Justice when order was restored in the Capital) no one really knew what the situation was in many places. But as the Army – now being adequately reinforced in spite of the difficulties which India had imposed on the process – fanned out from its bases, more information came in about the frightful atrocities committed by Awami League hooligans upon innocent persons. A brief summary of these terrible massacres will be found in Appendix No. 7; but no pen could do justice to their ghastly nature as shown by the photographs taken by the Army authorities. Rooms splashed ceiling high with blood and carpeted with corpses; pariah dogs and crows feeding on the dead; men, women and even small children hurriedly shovelled into mass graves; bloodstained dolls and toys pathetically testifying to the fate of their baby owners – these were some of the sights which the Army met when at length they overcame the obstacles of blocked roads, blown-up bridges, and water-transport destroyed. Of the mutineers of the East Bengal Regiment and the East Pakistan Rifles who joined the Awami League in the rebellion after they had shot many of their non-Bengali officers, it was said that they killed most of their victims cleanly; but the bestial fury of the mobs, turning upon non-Bengalis and even on Bengalis suspected of being but luke-warm supporters of the League, knew no restraint.

Of these massacres certain things need to be noted. First, the beginnings of them date from early March although the full fury of those who perpetrated them was not unleashed until 'D Day' in the early hours of March 26. Next, the evidence for them does not rest upon official records alone. In the beginning of April, a T V team which had come to Jessore under Awami League auspices when the town was still in rebel hands, filmed a typical example of the cold-blooded killings of Biharis, West Pakistanis and other non-Bengali citizens. Next, there is the evidence of British and Continental businessmen, in places like Chittagong, who had either refused, or were unable, to accept the advice of their own Consulates and Embassies to leave Pakistan in the early weeks of March. For the most part, they were not molested personally during the early period, although several of them had frightful tales to tell of the massacre of their factory hands, of the burnings of property, and of mob fury. But after 'D Day' things changed; many of them said frankly that only the arrival of the troops saved their lives.

It was this campaign of genocide perpetrated by the Awami League mobs, and not, as the time-table of event shows, the action of the Army, which set in motion the flood of refugees seeking food, safety and shelter across the Indian border. A highly disciplined force like the Pakistan Army rarely gets out of hand, even when confronted by evidence of murder, rape and mutilation perpetrated on innocent civilians. Such occasional acts of personal vengeance as occurred were, I am informed by the competent authorities, dealt with by the full severity of military law. Even so, the wildest stories of indiscriminate killing by the Army were carefully propagated by the Awami League and by the supporters of 'Bangla Desh' and conveyed to the outside world by every medium of mass-communication. They served to augment the fears of ordinary folk, and to swell the tide of fleeing refugees. Along with the innocent went many who had good reason to be afraid of the consequences to themselves of the restoration of Government authority – the broken remnants of the mutineers from the East Bengal Regiment and the East Pakistan Rifles, the Awami League leaders who had instituted a reign of terror in their own localities, and the revolting Razakars – Border guards – who had betrayed the trust imposed in them. The hard core of these elements was carefully separated from the rest by the Indian authorities, and directed into special training camps where in instruction in sabotage and infiltration was given to them. The existence of these camps have been vouched for by Western correspondents by no means unfriendly to India; it probably accounts for India's refusal to accept United Nations observers in the Border area – a suggestion that Pakistan, which had nothing to hide, promptly accepted.

Within a few weeks, overt resistance had been overcome by the Army; but the Pakistan Government were reluctant to make known to the outside world, the terrible story of what had happened during the Awami League's reign of terror. There are many East Pakistanis of Bengali race living in West Pakistan; there were battalions of the East Bengal Regiment stationed there who behaved perfectly. There has been much intermarriage between families living in either Wing; many of our West Pakistani friends have East Pakistani relations, and vice versa. The Government was afraid that if the full story of the terror was published, there might be massive reprisals against Bengali residents in the West. Strict censorship avoided this danger; but it also left Pakistan vulnerable to the accusations, carefully propagated by her enemies, that the atrocities occurring in East Pakistan were the work of the Army and not of the Awami League mobs. When my wife and I were in West Pakistan in July, we heard terrible stories from personal friends of what had happened to their relatives in East Pakistan. But by that time, their emotions were those of grief at their loss of sons, daughters, nephews and nieces, coupled with deep mourning, for child-relatives killed or maimed for life, rather than of a desire for revenge. Thus the policy of releasing information only gradually about the East Pakistan massacres achieved the desired ends; there were no reprisals against people of Bengali race living in the West Wing. But the price paid in damage to Pakistan's 'image' abroad was heavy.

Chapter 5   Pakistan, India and the World

S O U R C E S *Ian Stephens* Pakistan

Rushbrook Williams The State of Pakistan

Kemal A. Farukhi India's Role in the East Pakistan Crisis; and analysis of legal and political aspects.

Pakistan Institute of International Affairs May 1971

Ever since 1947, Pakistan has been deeply conscious that influential sections of Indian opinion have resented the mere fact of her existence, and have made no secret of their hope that the entire sub-continent will one day be reunited under the rule of New Delhi. Pakistan is determined to survive; many people in India wants her to break up. This fundamental difference of outlook underlies and exacerbates the serious disputes which have arisen between the two countries over Kashmir, riparian rights, boundary demarcations, anti-Muslim riots of considerable severity in Indian States, and variations in respective international alignments. East Pakistan, because of the predominance of the Bengali element in its population, because of its very considerable Hindu minority of some 15%, and because of its physical separation from West Pakistan by hundreds of miles of Indian territory has for long afforded favourable conditions for the exercise of Indian influence. The long-standing ties between the Hindus of East Pakistan and their coreligionists in Calcutta continued after partition; this ethnic element in the population has always regarded its incorporation in the polity of Pakistan as a temporary inconvenience. Successive Governments of Pakistan have long been aware of this; their policy has been to encourage the people of East Pakistan to develop a pride in being Pakistanis by giving them tangible evidence of the benefits which federation with other Provinces of the Republic can confer upon them. As has been pointed out in an earlier chapter, considerable progress has been made in overcoming the backwardness to which many centuries of neglect and exploitation had condemned East Pakistan. But impatience at the natural failure 'to build Rome in a day' fostered in some minds the belief, encouraged by pro-Indian influence, that it was only the sinister designs of West Pakistan which hampered the fulfilment of East Pakistani ambitions. This belief, although contradicted by facts, became an article of faith in the Awami League's creed.

The campaign conducted by Sheikh Mujibur Rahman and his Awami League followers in preparation for the 1970 elections was warmly supported from India, where his steady refusal to condemn Indian policies and actions which were reprobated throughout the rest of Pakistan were noted with satisfaction. His demand for maximum autonomy for East Pakistan was obviously on the right lines from India's point of view; and things seemed to be going so well that on March 2, 1971, an official spokesman of the External Affairs Ministry in New Delhi was reported by All-India Radio as saying that India regarded the developments in Pakistan as purely an internal affair of that country. But the Government of Pakistan found difficulty in taking this statement at its face value. They were convinced that India was in fact deeply concerned to foster a separatist movement in East Pakistan citing in evidence the 'stage-managed' hijacking incident leading to the ban on overflying; the heavy concentrations both of Indian Regular forces and Border Security Guards near the East Pakistan frontier; the constant communication across this frontier between Awami League Supporters and their sympathizers in West Bengal; and the steady flow of arms and munitions into the League's hands. The Pakistan Government are firmly convinced that without Indian countenance and backing, the militants of the Awami League would never have decided to resort to armed rebellion. As has been mentioned on an earlier page, President Yahya Khan hoped to the very last moment that reason would prevail, and that the Awami League would co-operate in his plans for the peaceful transfer of power.

When this hope was belied by the march of events, and the President was obliged to call upon the Army to restore order, the reaction from the Indian side was immediate. In the Lok Sabha, the Indian Prime Minister herself expressed her confidence in the triumph of 'the historical upsurge of 75 million people of East Bengal' and called up the governments of the world to induce Pakistan to stop 'the systematic decimation of people which amounts to genocide'. Indians, she asserted, could not remain indifferent to the macabre tragedy being enacted close to their border. All over the country, leading politicians and organizations of many kinds began raising funds to buy arms for the 'freedom fighters'; and influential voice were raised to assert that Sheikh Mujibur Rahman was 'fighting India's battle'; that the break-up of Pakistan is in our interest and we have an opportunity the like of which will never come again'. This last statement emanated from the Director of the Indian Institute for Defence Studies, and deserves notice for its frankness. There were many demands, which the Indian Government shrewdly evaded, for the immediate recognition of 'Bangla Desh' as an independent State; but they countenanced the presence of a 'shadow' administration, calling itself the 'Bangla Desh Government' in Calcutta; and they stepped up the supply of arms and the training of saboteurs to assist the insurgents in East Pakistan.

As the Pakistan Army advanced to restore order in district after district, the Awami League leaders sought refuge in India in increasing numbers. They brought with them the wildest stories of the triumphs of the 'freedom fighters' and the defeats of the Pakistan Army. These stories were not always consistent; while some said that peaceful and unarmed demonstrators had been 'mown down' by Army tanks, others related how these same demonstrators, in a fury of righteous indignation, had stormed Government House in Dacca and slain General Tikka Khan. (No one, apparently, was tactless enough to ask how a soldier of great experience, who was also Martial Law Administrator, had allowed himself to be caught napping in this way.) There were also many horrifying tales of the 'genocide' perpetrated by the Pakistan Army; no doubt those who related them could give gory details drawn from their own experience of the treatment which they had meted out to their political opponents and to the non-Bengalis in their power during the brief reign of terror which they had instituted. Many of these allegations of atrocities ascribed to the Army were broadcast to the world by some of the foreign journalists who had been expelled from East Pakistan and were now operating from India; some at least of them appear to have accepted as gospel truth all that they were told by the Indian authorities and by Awami League leaders who had sought sanctuary across the frontier. In the early days of the Army's advance, when certain districts of East Pakistan were still under Awami League control, some of these journalists visited these districts under Awami League auspices. Some of them even witnessed the massacre by Awami League supporters of their opponents, real or imaginary. But these terrible happenings were explained away as being a 'revenge' for atrocities committed by the Army in other places; the 'genocidal' aspect of the killings and mutilations attracted little attention.

Perhaps the most tragic element in the whole situation was the presence on Indian soil of large numbers of refugees from East Pakistan. There is some evidence that to begin with, India encouraged this exodus as providing material for her psychological campaign against Pakistan in the world's capitals by ascribing their plight to the brutal suppression by the Pakistan Army of a free, democratic movement. In fact, the time-table shows that the movement began before the Army took action at all; for the most part it was an endeavour to get away from the violence and confusion, and the disturbance of all ordered life, resulting from the Awami League's usurpation of authority in East Pakistan from the beginning of March 1971.

The terrible overpopulation of East Pakistan, and the pressure on the soil makes her people very dependent upon imported food-stuffs. The Awami League's methodical destruction of roads, bridges, boats and all ordinary means of communication cut off the flow of these food supplies, leaving masses of people with no other course than to cross the Indian border in the hope of finding sustenance. To these were added as has already been noted in another page, the broken remnants of the rebellious forces, many 'committed' supporters of the Awami League, including a good number of members elected to the National Assembly and the Provincial Legislature, many Border Guards, and fresh streams of genuine refugees moving away from the areas where clashes between the Pakistan Army and surviving pockets of resistance to it were causing disturbances. Conditions in the refugee camps set up by the Indian Government soon became pitiable in the extreme. That Government, finding the numbers of refugees an embarrass-ment, appealed to the humanitarian sentiment of the world to assist them in the task of looking after their camps, while at the same time indicting the Government of Pakistan as the sole author of all the suffering. A continuous stream of propaganda emanated from the West Bengal Press and from All India Radio, encouraging poor, simple persons to flee from the awful fate which the advancing Pakistan Army was about to mete out to them. This in its turn contributed to the confusion in East Pakistan and swelled the numbers crossing the Indian frontier. As might have been expected, Awami League supporters and other elements hostile to the Pakistan Government lent additional venom to this propaganda, which enjoyed wide currency both in India and in many Western countries, thanks in some measure to some foreign newspaper correspondents. As to the number of refugees actually involved in this mass-movement, it is impossible to speak with any accuracy. It was to the advantage of the Indian authorities to inflate their numbers in order to encourage assistance from foreign Governments, relief organizations, and private charity. From an initial estimate of 2 to 3 millions, the figure publicized by India steadily mounted, until the wholly incredible statement that refugees were crossing the border at the rate of 1 million a day was put out. What seems quite certain is that a considerable proportion of those in the refugee camps did not come from East Pakistan; it is known, for example, that enormous numbers of indigent people from Calcutta and its environs flocked to nearby camps, attracted by the prospect of free food, free shelter, and assistance from foreign sources. Something similar, but on a far smaller scale, had happened during the cyclone relief operations in East Pakistan, when Dacca was almost emptied of professional mendicants who made their way to the camps primarily intended for the victims of the cyclone.

There seems little doubt that the Indian authorities made great efforts to feed and shelter the refugees to guard against epidemics, and to procure substantial quantities of foreign relief. These efforts were broadcast to the world. Thanks to her very efficient machinery, both external and internal, of public relations, it was not difficult for India to represent herself to the world as an unselfish humanitarian Power, primarily interested in mitigating an appalling human catastrophe. What must strike the outside observer as less admirable is the astute use which she made of this posture to promote her aim of breaking up Pakistan by encouraging to the utmost of her ability the creation of a separate 'Bangla Desh' out of the Eastern wing. Apart from giving countenance to the 'shadow government' which Awami League exiles set up in Calcutta, India actively promoted the campaign of murder and sabotage which the so-called 'freedom fighters', using her territory and her training camps as their bases and sanctuaries, proceeded to conduct inside East Pakistan. The main sufferers from this campaign were not the Pakistan Government or the Pakistan Army, but the masses of poor folk whose way of life depended upon the availability of imported foodstuffs, the resumption of normal cultivation, and the restoration of communications between Chittagong, Khulna, and other centres where bulk supplies from West Pakistan and from foreign countries were arriving, and the outlying areas where these supplies were badly needed.

When my wife and I were in East Pakistan in July 1971, at the height of the monsoon, the Army's job of restoring order was virtually finished; but all the troops were working desperately hard to mend the roads and bridges, and to replace the small boats, which the Awami League had destroyed. At that time, there was enough food in the country to last until the end of September, the difficulty was to distribute it. The job of restoring communications was much hampered by fresh acts of sabotage committed by infiltrators from India; these men did not care what damage they did to bridges, dams, power plants, and public utility undertakings so long as they were hindering the Army and the civil authorities in the task of restoring normal conditions. To the outside world, these outrages were represented as the brave exploits of 'freedom fighters' striving for the independence of 'Bangla Desh' against a soulless, repressive military tyranny. But, as we ourselves quickly found, the people who suffered from these irresponsible acts did not see things in that light at all; their one anxiety was that disturbances should cease so that they could resume cultivation, small trading, and the other activities of normal life. In Dacca and other big cities, this was rapidly being achieved; we found that the wives and children of British and foreign businessmen were already coming back to rejoin their husbands and fathers. Incidentally, the business community were quite uninhibited in expressing their views to us; in their judgment, President Yahya Khan's action in calling in the Army was the only thing that had saved East Pakistan from complete anarchy; their criticism was that he did not do this sooner. They were very angry indeed at the way that the situation was being misrepresented, as they saw it, in the British Press and by the B B C – which some of them nicknamed '*Bharat* (India) Broadcasting Corporation'. It was the Army, they asserted, that had saved their lives, their factories, their places of business, their tea-gardens; and they did not care who heard them say it. Similar sentiments were expressed, if more politely, by many of the East Pakistani business community whom we met.

But whatever may have been the opinion of observers on the spot, who had seen with their own eyes the kind of things that were happening during the Awami League's reign of terror, the outside world was taking a very different view. The fact is that India was on a very good 'humanitarian' wicket, and she was determined to make the most of her advantage. Numerous delegations, Parliamentary and otherwise, from Western countries were invited to visit the refugee camps. To men and women unfamiliar with the deplorably low living-standards current in East Pakistan and West Bengal, the sight of these unfortunates, and the conditions in which they were living, was a shattering experience. Ignorant of the language, and dependent for their information upon the services of Indian or Awami League interpreters, many of these well-meaning visitors accepted uncritically the assertions that all this suffering was the result of the cruel action of the military régime in Pakistan and of the Army which was the régime's instrument in repressing 'a democratic movement based upon free elections and the will of the people'. Moreover, they tended to support the Indian contention that the only way to relieve all this terrible suffering was to restore 'democratic' government in East Pakistan by bringing back to power Sheikh Mujibur Rahman and the Awami League, so that the refugees could safely return to their country. And the best way to do this, the visitors concluded, was to persuade their own Western Governments to bring every kind of pressure, moral, economic and financial, upon the Government of Pakistan to compel that Government to act in the desired manner. By the time that these amiable visitors came to Pakistan – which not all of them did – they had formed such decided views that they were unable to see that there might be another side to the whole Indo-Pakistani dispute. They had become, in effect, partisan of the Indian attitude and of 'Bangla Desh'. My wife and I had the opportunity of talking to some of them; we found only a few who suspected that Pakistan had a case which they had not yet heard, and were ready to suspend judgment until they had heard it.

Nor did the Indian Government rely only upon the supply of tendentious information by foreign correspondents and by their own Press and mass-media; their Foreign Minister, Sardar Swaran Singh, made a tour of the principal capitals to ensure that the Indian point of view was represented effectively in the highest quarters. Initially, the reaction of most Western Governments to the tragic events in East Pakistan was to regard them, quite correctly, as an internal affair which was Pakistan's own business and nobody else's. This attitude was consistently maintained by the Governments of the Arab· World, of the South East Asian countries, of the Chinese People's Republic, and of Pakistan's partners on the Regional Cooperation for Development organization, Turkey and Iran. Another Government which, if my information is correct, refused to diverge from that line, was that of France. But before long, in the judgment of Pakistan at least, a change began to appear in the attitudes of certain Western countries, as powerful sections of opinion within them began to exert sustained pressure for some action against Pakistan to oblige her to 'make terms' and arrive at a 'political settlement' with Sheikh Mujibur Rahman and the Awami League. In the United States, the Democratic Party called for the cessation of all aid to Pakistan, whether in cash or kind, until the desired type of political settlement was reached. President Nixon's Administration resisted this pressure. In Canada, however, those who were bringing it to bear had greater success, and the attitude of the Government towards aid to Pakistan changed accordingly. But in the view of the Government of Pakistan, it is the outlook of Great Britain that has become the most unfriendly.

Before my wife and I arrived in Pakistan, for the second time in 1971, early in July, we had no idea of this; we were deeply shocked by the grief and anger displayed by so many of our Pakistani friends, both inside and outside the Government. In their view, both Mr. Heath and Sir Alec Douglas-Home had departed from their original statements that the tragedy of East Pakistan was a domestic affair. They accused the British Government of taking the lead in stopping all fresh aid to Pakistan, and persuading other Governments to follow the same line until a 'settlement acceptable to all parties in East Pakistan" is arrived at. Our Pakistani friends told us that they did not expect Britain to agree in all respects with the Pakistani point of view, but they did expect, in light of the old friendly relations between the two countries, that Britain would at least display impartiality in the face of Indo-Pakistani differences. They accused the British of giving Pakistan a series of deliberate snubs; first by the issue of the communiqué after the talks between the British Foreign and Commonwealth Secretary and Sardar Swaran Singh, referring to India's 'restraint' – which seemed to Pakistan a peculiarly unfortunate description of India's entire attitude; next, by taking a leading part in the movement by Pakistan's enemies to cut off all fresh aid; thirdly, by insisting upon a 'political settlement' (as though President Yahya Khan had ever contemplated anything else); and finally by slandering the Pakistan Army by attributing to it the sole responsibility for the atrocities and persecutions which had set in motion the flood of refugees.

The feeling against Britain was, we found, so bitter that men who for all their lives had valued British friendship, who were immensely grateful for the way in which British soldiers and administrators had helped Pakistan to surmount the difficulties of her early years, and who had highly valued the Commonwealth connection, were now taking the lead in demanding that their country should leave the Commonwealth.

On reflection, we did not find it difficult to understand this point of view; for the attitude of the British Press and of the mass-media has been, on the whole, so consistently hostile to President Yahya Khan's Government, that the Pakistan case has never been given a proper hearing; indeed the President's carefully prepared, frank and factual 'reports to the nation' have been dismissed in a few lines, while every statement from the Indian side has been given great prominence. To my own mind, there are several explanations of this fact, none of which, I fear, will go far to assuage the present anti-British feeling in Pakistan. The first is the existence in London since the early days of the India League in the pre-independence period, of a powerful 'Indian Lobby' supported by liberal and democratic sentiment and reinforced by the almost charismatic status to which Mr. Gandhi and the Nehru family have been elevated. To many of those who hold these views, the very existence of Pakistan is anathema, as a rent in the seamless garment of Mother India. Secondly, there exists in Britain – and no doubt it must be counted among that country's tiltes to fame – a body of opinion which instinctively supports almost any claim, no matter how dubious in essence, put forward by a group of people who assert that they are being oppressed. It was this body of opinion who supported the ill-fated claim to independence by Biafra; they turned a ready ear to the protagonists of 'Bangla Desh'. Collectively, their influence is considerable, especially in intellectual circles which are traditionally left-wing in outlook; and they command a ready hearing in the Press, on radio, and on television.

A further factor in the formation of British public opinion, at least as reflected in the mass-media, has been the presence in the United

Kingdom of considerable numbers of East Pakistanis. Not by any means all of them support 'Bangla Desh'; many indeed are firmly loyal to Pakistan as founded by Quaid-i-Azam Mohammed Ali Jinnah. But among the student community, in particular, the cause of 'Bangla Desh' aroused great enthusiasm, and attracted many very vocal supporters. As has been already explained, the Awami League got away with a great deal of money; from this and from other sources, there was no shortage of funds. 'Bangla Desh' offices were set up in several parts of the United Kingdom; a former justice of the Dacca High Court, who had come to England with his family, set up a 'High Commission' for 'Bangla Desh'. Full page advertisements were displayed in certain national newspapers, bearing the names of numerous Members of Parliament associated with liberal and humanitarian causes, calling for support for the 'oppressed people of Bangla Desh'. These advertisements, it need hardly be said, conveniently omitted to mention the cardinal fact that Sheikh Mujibur Rahman and the Awami League had won the elections, not on the platform of an independent 'Bangla Desh', but on a plan for provincial autonomy within the structure of a federal Pakistan. Nor did they mention the atrocities which League supporters had perpetrated during their usurpation of authority. Of all this activity some was undoubtedly counter-productive, provoking loyal Pakistanis in the United Kingdom to demonstrations of attachment to their country and to vigorous protests against attempts, whether by Britain, India or anyone else, to interfere in its domestic affairs. But Pakistanis in Pakistan might well be pardoned for thinking that the entire public opinion of Britain, with the tacit approval of the Government, was solidly ranged against them.

This was not, of course, true; Pakistan has many loyal friends in Britain, particularly among those who have worked in the country, who know the difficulties which it has had to overcome, and have seen with their own eyes the rapid progress which has been made in East Pakistan as well as in other parts of the country in economic development, both industrial and agricultural, and in sound financial administration. But Pakistan has never been able, or perhaps has never cared, to afford the cost of the very efficient machinery of public relations of the kind which India has established in Western countries. Although the various Pakistan Embassies and High Commissions did their best to counter the flood of propaganda which was blackening the good name of their country, few of them were able to command the costly services of people with practical experience of what has become a highly professional vocation. In consequence, the friends of Pakistan, in Britain at any rate, lacked detailed material to counter the campaign conducted by the 'India Lobby', by the fanatical supporters of 'Bangla Desh', and, perhaps above all, by those deeply moved by purely humanitarian sympathy for the plight of the refugees, who took the easy course of blaming the Pakistan Government for causing the entire tragedy. The existence of the refugee camps, in fact, became the most potent weapon in India's armoury of psychological warfare; it was used mercilessly in the British Press and on radio and television to arouse bitter criticism of the Government over which President Yahya Khan presided. It was the more effective for two reasons: first, the deplorable condition of the refugees was a fact that no one could deny. Secondly, the Awami League's pre-election propaganda about the alleged failure of the Pakistan Government to cope adequately with the aftermath of the great cyclone disaster, false as it was, had created the impression that the Government were less deeply concerned with the misfortunes of East Pakistan than the situation demanded. Nothing had been further from the truth; but the damaging impression had not been eliminated. By way of contrast to this, India's manifest concern, publicized throughout the world, for the welfare of the refugees who had flocked across her border, won for her much support in 'liberal' and humanitarian sections of opinion. This support was intensified as the monsoon of 1971, with its devastating floods and inundations, aggravated the already unhappy condition of the refugees in West Bengal and the population of many districts in East Pakistan.

These latter became in their turn the object of great sympathy, and the direct prophecies about the fate which was likely to overtake them became current in the British Press. The exploits of the 'freedom fighters' in interrupting communications, and in hindering the transport of food where it was needed, became the occasion for fresh demands that President Yahya Khan's Government should be 'pressurised' into making terms with the Awami League so that the distribution of food and other necessities could take place unhindered. This course of action was strongly pressed by India, who claimed that she was unable to control the 'freedom fighters' operating from her territory, and that the shadow 'Bangla Desh' Government and the Awami League were the only people to deal with. That this specious excuse for inaction on India's part should have carried conviction in certain quarters in Britain is all the more curious in light of that country's recent experience in Northern Ireland, where branches of the Irish Republican Army, from the safety of the Republic of Eire, conduct a campaign of murder and sabotage from which British troops (like the Pakistan Army in East Pakistan) attempt to protect the civil population. In each case, too, the country which gives shelter to the miscreants has an admitted interest in upsetting existing political arrangements.

In the Super-Power alignments over the East Pakistan tragedy, some interesting developments may be noted. From the first, the People's Republic of China strongly supported the Government of Pakistan, giving very useful aid in food grains, in badly-needed river craft, and even going so far as to warn India against interfering in her neighbour's affairs – much to India's indignation. No doubt because of this alignment, the Soviet Union, which values its ties both with India and with Pakistan, at first seemed inclined to take the Indian view, sending a message (which Pakistan, in her turn, resented) pressing President Yahya Khan to work for a 'political settlement'. But later on, in June to be exact, there were signs that the Soviet Union was changing its position a little. The joint communiqué issued after Mr. Kosygin's visit to Delhi now called for a political solution which would 'answer the interests of the entire people of Pakistan'. No mention of East Pakistani separatism, still less of 'Bangla Desh'! This development was received with great indignation by the shadow government of 'Bangla Desh' and by the Awami League exiles in India, but attracted comparatively little attention elsewhere, where interest was concentrated on the new Indo-Soviet treaty of friendship. So far as the United States are concerned, mention has been made of the fact that President Nixon did not yield to the demand that aid to Pakistan should be cut off. In fact, it continued, helped by Pakistan's willingness to admit United Nations observers, to accept the loan of coastal vessels with mixed Pakistani and foreign crews to distribute food in East Pakistan, and to permit American and United Nations officials to cooperate in working relief programmes. The United States were completely satisfied that President Yahya Khan would never be the first to start hostilities with India and her ties with Pakistan were strengthened by the part which that country played in arranging Dr. Kissinger's super-secret journey to Peking in July

1971 to pave the way for President Nixon's own visit in the near future.

This diplomatic *coup* was executed in masterly fashion. When my wife and I arrived at Islamabad airport in July, we knew, like everyone else in Pakistan, that Dr. Kissinger was visiting President Yahya Khan; and we saw his special plane standing by on the apron. It was given out that Dr. Kissinger was suffering from overwork and an upset stomach – a common complaint among foreign visitors to Pakistan – and that he had gone to the cooler climate of Nathia Gali – where the President of Pakistan occasionally uses the modest house which was once the summer residence of Governors of the North-West Frontier Province in British times. No one saw anything strange about this. What actually happened was known only to a handful of people. Dr. Kissinger, taking advantage of the fact that relations between Islamabad and Peking are cordial, and that Pakistan International Airlines maintain a regular service between Pakistan and the People's Republic of China, had slipped away to conduct his delicate mission on behalf of President Nixon. He returned with the same secrecy that had marked his departure; he landed not in Islamabad airport, but in Peshawar, whence he was flown back to his plane, still in Islamabad, by helicopter. Not until Washington released the news did the world know what had happened and that a new era in the troubled relations between the United States and China had begun.

The Pakistan Government were naturally very pleased that that their good offices had proved successful; they have long been working for the admission of the People's Republic to its rightful place in the United Nations; and Dr. Kissinger's visit seemed to bring closer that important event. Moreover, the United States had begun to understand Pakistan's viewpoint in relation to the East Pakistan tragedy, and was in a position to give valuable help. In the history of international diplomacy, there can have been few secrets better kept than that of Dr. Kissinger's flight to Peking; and although, while he was away, my wife and I had intimate talks with many people, including the President himself, in Islamabad and Rawalpindi, we were as surprised as everyone else when the news 'broke'. By an odd coincidence, the P I A plane in which we flew back to Britain after our July/August visit to Pakistan was the same machine that had carried Dr. Kissinger; in addition to the usual posted notices to passengers in Urdu,

Bengali and English, a line or two in Chinese ideographs had been written.

The prospect of enhanced American and United Nations co-operation with the Pakistan Government in rehabilitating the economy of East Pakistan and repairing the damage inflicted by the rebellion was most unwelcome to the Awami League exiles, since it threatened to curtail the use of their main weapon against the Pakistan Government, namely, the disruption by sabotage and violence of the network of communications essential for the distribution of food and other necessities to areas in need of relief. With characteristic ruthlessness and disregard of all humane considerations, Awami League spokesmen announced that all relief workers co-operating with the Government and the Army would be treated as enemies and that they would be appropriately dealt with by the 'freedom fighters'. It remains to be seen whether the 'shadow government' of 'Bangla Desh' and its adherents will put this threat into execution; but their brutal treatment of non-Bengalis and of their political opponents during their brief reign of terror in March and April 1971 seems to make it not unlikely. It may be noted in passing that the attitude of the Indian authorities towards relief workers has varied from time to time. While relief funds and medical supplies have been welcomed, restrictions of one kind or another have been placed on the movements of foreign relief workers, and they have been removed from certain of the refugee camps near some places on the Indo-Pakistani frontier; sometimes on the pretext that they have been 'spying' and sometimes on the grounds that they may be killed by 'Maoist' and 'Naxalite' elements in the locality. What is quite clear, as is shown by India's refusal to allow United Nations observers in the border areas – although they would have been welcomed by Pakistanis that India cannot afford to allow her frontier activities, and her training camps for saboteurs, to be exposed to the scrutiny of foreign observers.

No doubt, the unsettled conditions in West Bengal, the bitter fighting between rival political parties, and the recurrent mob violence and murder in Calcutta and throughout the countryside, have all played their part in her decision. But there are many people still in western countries and particularly in Britain, who firmly hold that India can do no wrong and that everything that she says and does in connection with the affairs of East Pakistan is inspired by the highest and most altruistic motives.

In many lands this attitude is beginning to lose its plausibility; and as 1971 draws to a close, there are signs that Pakistan's version of the dispute is beginning to attract some notice. But this has not prevented the British Labour Party, to take one example, from pressing the British Government to urge the Pakistan Government to release Sheikh Mujibur Rahman and to bring the situation in East Pakistan to the notice of the United Nations on the grounds that it constitutes a threat to peace. Until now, India has appeared unwilling to bring the United Nations into the quarrel, no doubt foreseeing the strong support which Pakistan would be likely to receive from the entire Muslim world as well as from many other quarters in her contention that the affairs of East Pakistan are matters domestic to herself.

Chapter 6   After the Rebellion: Political Reconstruction

S O U R C E S   *White Paper on the Crisis in East Pakistan*
(Government Publication)
President's Speeches of March and June 1971
Press Conference in July 1971

As has already been related on earlier pages, the actions of the Awami League in paralysing normal administration, overawing or murdering opponents, and setting up their own 'parallel government' necessitated serious changes in the time-table which President Yahya Khan had proposed for transferring power to democratically-elected National and Provincial Assemblies. In surveying the events of March 1971 in East Pakistan, it is difficult for the detached observer to escape the conclusion that Sheikh Mujibur Rahman and the League badly overplayed their originally strong hand when they allowed self-confidence to outweigh political judgment. By indulging in the massacre of opponents and pogroms against non-Bengalis, they reduced the Province to virtual anarchy. Even so, it is clear from the official record that if they had displayed even a modicum of readiness to co-operate with the other federating elements which were to be their partners in shaping the new democratic constitution of the Islamic Republic -- as they themselves, by accepting the Legal Framework Order as the basis for the elections had pledged themselves to do -- it would have been wholly unnecessary for them to put into operation their plans for seizing power by force. The President has shown, time after time, that as a soldier who knows all too well what fighting entails in misery and suffering, he is a firm adherent of Sir Winston Churchill's conviction that 'Jaw, Jaw' is far superior to 'War, War' as a method of resolving political issues. It was not the President who broke off the talks with the League. It was only when it became clear to him, after their arrogantly-worded ultimatum, that they were on the point of putting into operation their carefully-contrived plans for an armed rising that he took the action which has been so widely misrepresented in the Press of the western world. Up to this eleventh hour, as it were, the Army had been restrained from effective intervention by the stringent orders which he himself had imposed upon it. He had now no other course open to him than to use it to restore the authority of the Government over those who were on the verge of launching civil war.

The partisans of 'Bangla Desh' lost no time in publicising their own version of how and why the talks in Dacca broke down; it was only when the Government of Pakistan published, in August, the White Paper on East Pakistan that the true course of events were made public. In the absence of the official record, the President's critics were able to indulge their fancy in the way which they considered most favourable to their cause. He was even accused of himself proposing that the National Assembly should sit in two parts, one for the West and one for the East, Wing – which is the very last thing that he would ever dream of doing, holding as he does that his main duty is to preserve the polity of Pakistan as Quaid-i-Azam bequeathed it. Another accusation is brought against him; he is alleged to have 'spun out' the Dacca negotiations in order to gain time to reinforce the slender strength of the Army units in East Pakistan, in preparation for the 'show-down' which he is accused of planning. Again, this charge lacks foundation. Ever since he was called to power in March 1969, President Yahya Khan has steadily pursued the aim of handing over authority to a democratically-elected régime and of withdrawing martial law. It would appear most improbable that he should completely reverse this policy on the spur of the moment. Further, the unhindered escape of all the most prominent Awami League leaders, with the exception of the Sheikh himself, to the sanctuary kindly provided for them by India argues strongly against the possibility of any properly-planned military *coup* by the President, which would assuredly have included provision for arresting the persons of those guilty of planning rebellion. Finally, if my own information is correct, Army reinforcements from West Pakistan were only able to arrive after, and not before, the President took action. Indeed, it was essential to the success of the Awami League's plan that the reception-areas should be seized as a first step, precisely to prevent such reinforcements arriving. Had the President's action been planned in advance, as his critics allege, these fresh troops would assuredly have been brought in earlier. As was made clear on another page, the Awami League's hopes that the Indian ban on over-flying would prevent this operation proved wholly illusory, and they were obliged to do all that they could to hinder it after, and not before, their planned military uprising.

Even before open resistance to Governmental authority had been broken, the President made it clear, in his speech of March 26 that his intention of transferring power to the representatives of the people remained unaltered by the necessity, which events had forced upon him, of banning political activity for the time being, imposing Press censorship, and completely banning the Awami League as a political party. He promised that as soon as the situation permitted, he would take fresh steps to enable the transfer of power to be achieved. By the end of June, 1971 he and his advisers had evolved a programme to meet the new situation. It was essential, he said, that the activities of some misguided persons should not be allowed to frustrate the results of the first real elections ever held in Pakistan. Although the Awami League as a party had been banned, members of the National Assembly and of the Provincial Assembly would be allowed to retain their seats; the only people who would be banned were those who had taken a leading part in criminal or anti State activities. A list of these guilty persons would, the President announced, be published in the near future; their seats would be declared vacant and would be filled in the ordinary way through by-elections. The President called upon all members of the Awami League who had nothing to do with secessionist policies to come forward and play their part in reconstructing the political life of East Pakistan. He announced a new approach to the problem of forming a constitution, which he considered, in light of past experience, to be over-difficult for a National Assembly which must at the same time ensure that urgent social and economic problems are not neglected. He therefore proposed to set experts to work to produce a constitution embodying the principles which had already become generally accepted; Islamic ideology; full social and economic justice to all sections of society; federal institutions; maximum autonomy, legislative, administrative and financial, for the Provinces which is compatible with the Federal Government powers to discharge its domestic and foreign responsibilities and to maintain the integrity of the country. According to this plan, the National Assembly would not have to function as a constituent assembly as well; as soon as it met, it would become the Central Legislature forthwith. It would be able to modify the constitution, should it want to do this, by procedures laid down for the purpose. The President rejected the idea that power ought not to be transferred to elected representatives until complete normalcy was restored; on the contrary, he thought that normalcy would not be achieved until these representatives assumed responsibility for the administration. He hoped, therefore, that the transfer of power could take place as soon as the basic infrastructure of law and order had gained full strength – which he believed would be possible in about four months' time.

In the same broadcast the President, following his previous practice, gave the nation a full and frank account of Pakistan's problems, both domestic and foreign, and called upon every section of the community to work hard in solving them. One portion of his speech was particularly relevant to the attempt, briefly described on an earlier page, of certain foreign countries to induce his Government, under the threat of depriving Pakistan of foreign aid, to make terms with Sheikh Mujibur Rahman and 'Bangla Desh'. President Yahya Khan expressed his gratitude for the help which had been given in the past, but made it quite clear his country would accept no aid which carried 'strings' making inroads into its sovereignty and trying to enforce a political set-up of a particular kind. In making this statement, as I can testify from personal experience, he was speaking the mind of practically every Pakistani to whom I talked in July and August. Even those East Pakistanis who thought that Sheikh Mujibur Rahman, having learned his lesson, should be brought back to power as the best way of restoring peaceful progress in East Pakistan, were bitterly resentful of what they saw as the efforts of India – and, I am sorry to have to say, of Britain, too – to interfere in Pakistan's domestic affairs. In another passage, the President spoke very frankly about India's part in inflaming the situation in East Pakistan, indicting her not only for helping the secessionists with men and material, but also for launching 'a malicious campaign of falsehood' against Pakistan through the Indian radio and Press.

No one, I think, who knows the real facts can deny that India has immeasurably increased Pakistan's difficulties in dealing with the situation in East Pakistan. Some of the methods which she has used for doing this have already been described in earlier pages; but it is necessary now to consider her deliberate provocation of tension along the East Pakistan frontier, and the use that she made of the tension so created to arouse the fear of western countries that Pakistan was about to resort to war – a war which might produce incalculable consequences because the Super Powers might be drawn in. There is a school of opinion among Indian publicists who hold that the threat of war, as opposed to its actual declaration, is a legitimate weapon.

In pursuance of this opinion, a number of people important in Indian political life let it be widely known abroad that India could not be expected to refrain for ever from intervening in East Pakistan in order to ensure that the East Pakistani refugees would be able safely to return, without molestation from anyone, to an independent 'Bangla Desh'. This point of view was pressed very hard in western countries in support of India's hope that their respective Governments would, for fear of the incalculable consequences to world peace if India was 'forced' into taking this action, bring effective pressure upon the Government of Pakistan to make terms with the Awami League and permit East Pakistan to break away. To what extent this threat was seriously intended may be open to question; certainly that distinguished and patriotic Bengali writer Mr. Nirad C. Chaudhuri could not believe, as he said, that the present Government of India, though he did not like them, would be so utterly mad as to do anything of the kind. But the mere threat itself served to help India's contention that the situation in East Pakistan was something in which the whole world ought to be interested – something that could not safely be left to the Pakistan Government to settle. It has been just as well for everyone that President Yahya Khan is a soldier. Unlike some politicians, soldiers do not contemplate war with equanimity; they know what it entails. So, from first to last, the Pakistan Government have played things very cool, even though Mrs. Indira Gandhi refused President Yahya Khan's suggestion that they should meet together and see if Indo-Pakistani relations could not be improved. The President was not discouraged by this rebuff, and later in 1971 made further efforts to bring his country and India to a better understanding by proposing that Iran and the Soviet Union should jointly mediate between them.

While India was sedulously representing to the world that her patience was running out and that she might be obliged to intervene actively in East Pakistan to create conditions in which the refugees would find it safe to return, her threat, sometimes veiled and sometimes open, of this kind of intervention was itself an active deterrent to any such movement on their part. So long as this talk of war was in the air, the refugees, no matter how pitiable might be the conditions in which they were living, would never dare to recross the frontier for fear of being caught in the cross-fire of hostilities. Further, apart altogether from the disquieting rumours of direct action which India was at pains to spread, the entire situation on the border was desperately uneasy. So long as Awami League partisans were able to put up any kind of show of resistance to the Pakistan Army, Indian rifles, machine guns and cartridges – many of which were captured and exhibited by the Pakistan authorities – poured across the border to assist the insurgents. This traffic was quite extensive; it was reported by several Western correspondents who were allowed by India to enter the border area so long as it seemed that the rebellion had a chance of success. When it became clear that the Army's action had eliminated this chance, the supply of arms ceased; and the next step from the Indian side was the infiltration into East Pakistan of personnel drawn from Indian Border Security Force battalions (the battalion-numbers of whom were identified by the Pakistan authorities) to encourage dissident elements and sabotage communications to impede the advance of the Army. The Army captured a number of them. In addition to Indian Border Security Force personnel, the East Pakistan border was regularly penetrated by former members of the East Bengal Regiment, the East Pakistan Rifles, and frontier guards. These men were collected into special training camps on the Indian side of the border, where they were given instruction in sabotage and guerilla warfare.

A certain number of them, it is fair to assume, are convinced partisans of 'Bangla Desh', ready and willing to do all that they can to carry on the struggle. Others, on the contrary, were at best half-hearted and had no wish at all to fight. In spite of the strict control which was kept over them, some of this latter group contrived to get away, and they gave details to the Pakistan authorities both of the kind of training that was being given, and of the pressure which had been brought to bear upon them to undergo it. Many of them had wives and families in the ordinary refugee camps; they were told that their dependants would draw no rations unless their own conduct was satisfactory. There can be little doubt that India placed great reliance on the unsettling effect which the guerilla operations organized from these training camps would produce in East Pakistan; and as these operations grew in strength and complexity, India began to impose more and more stringent restrictions upon 'outsiders', whether relief workers or foreign correspondents, who wished to move about the frontier areas.

Nor did India rely entirely upon Border Security Guards and East Pakistani partisans to maintain tension along the frontier. Even before trouble broke out in East Pakistan, that is to say, quite early in 1971, sizeable forces of the Indian Army had been stationed in West Bengal, where internal security presented difficult problems, especially in view of the forthcoming elections. When the elections were over, these forces were not withdrawn but were augmented, and some units were moved close to the border, those at Agartala being reported in considerable strength. In the estimation of the Pakistan authorities, so I was informed, more than five divisions of the Indian Army were stationed in West Bengal when the rising in East Pakistan was planned; while Indian Air Force stations along the western and northern borders of that Province were in a high state of combat readiness. It would appear that all this apparent military and para-military activity was designed to lend weight to Indian statements that India was all ready for action if she was 'compelled' to take it. Foreign correspondents in Delhi were encouraged to send despatches underlining the grave risk of an Indo-Pakistani war. Some of them, indeed, were allowed to report – a strange concession for the military to make to the Press – actual troop movements; as when the correspondent of the London *Times* disclosed on May 10 that at least three regiments from Northern India, the Punjab Regiment, the Rajputs, and the Mahratta Light Infantry, were in the vanguard on the Jessore front, with recoilless anti-tank guns, mounted on jeeps within 50 yards of the border, while Sikhs and Rajputs were to be seen constructing fortifications and dugouts along the disused railway line connecting India and 'East Bengal'.

It should be noted that India's action in stationing Regular forces so close to the frontier seems to be a deliberate reversal of the prudent practice, designed to reduce the risk of border clashes, hitherto adopted by both countries, namely, to keep the Regular Army units well back, and to rely on para-military frontier guards to perform actual patrolling duties. The Pakistan Government very soon began to complain of infringements of the border by Indian soldiers, to say nothing of guerilla fighters, and of repeated shelling of border villages on the Pakistan side. Until Pakistan's own system of border guards was reorganized – which happened remarkably quickly as the people of the areas concerned became more and more annoyed at Indian interference and flocked to enlist in the newly reconstituted Razakars and Ansars – the Pakistan Army was itself obliged to guard the frontier. But it was under the strictest orders not to start anything; when it was fired upon, it returned the fire but did nothing more. As President Yahya Khan himself said at the end of July 1971, such a situation would normally have meant war but he was trying to avoid it and showing a lot of patience; but that if India had any idea of 'taking a chunk of East Pakistan' he would fight to defend his country.

My own observations in East and West Pakistan during July and August 1971 have left me with the firm impression that the avoidance of open hostilities between Pakistan and India during that period should be credited to President Yahya Khan rather than to the Indian Government. He refused to be enticed into drastic action in face of a good deal of provocation from the Indian side. Pakistani ships were harassed by the Indian Navy in April; a new Indian ground-to-air missile base came into action with practice firing up to a range of 123 miles from India's southern tip, forcing Pakistan International Airlines civil aircraft to fly even farther South and increasing the length of the already stretched Karachi-Dacca flights. Moreover, when some of the staff of the Pakistan Deputy High Commission in Calcutta defected, the Indian Government refused to help the new Deputy High Commissioner to regain control of his premises. The Indian authorities helped exiled Awami League leaders to proclaim 'The Republic of Bangla Desh' at a spot a few yards inside East Pakistan territory – after which the leaders scuttled back to the safety of the State Guest House in Calcutta. The so-called 'Free Radio of Bangla Desh' operated, so Western correspondents found, along the beam, and from the premises, of All India Radio. To give shelter to political exiles is one thing; many countries of the world take pride in the liberality of their institutions which permits this to be done. But to allow these political exiles to organize and conduct openly hostile operations, to provide them with the means of doing this, and to co-operate actively with them in raiding the territory of a neighbour – this seems to me to be quite a different thing. And this, I cannot help concluding, is just what India does, on the pretext that she is concerned only to help the refugees and secure their return to an East Pakistan governed according to the plan which meets *her* approval, simply, I fear, because it is calculated to split up and weaken Pakistan.

Just as the ordinary people of East Pakistan are the worst sufferers from the campaign of murder, sabotage, and disruption of public utilities which India countenances and aids, so it is the refugees who find their plight worsened by circumstances of India's creation. As soon as law and order was restored in East Pakistan, the Pakistan Government lost no time in assuring the refugees that it was safe for them to return to their homes and that they would be given help in resuming their normal lives. On May 21, 1971 President Yahya Khan invited all bona fide Pakistan citizens to return home, urging them not to be misled by false propaganda directed against the Government. He repeated this assurance on May 24. At the same time, it was announced that reception centres were being set up to help returning refugees. In these centres, food, clothing and funds would be available to assist them to reach their homes and to start life again. Initially, nineteen centres were in operation; later on the number was raised to twenty-nine. In June 1971, an amnesty was extended to members of the East Bengal Regiment, the East Pakistan Rifles, and the Police who surrendered voluntarily; they would be allowed to rejoin their families and individual cases would be considered compassionately. In the same month the United Nations High Commissioner for Refugees visited a number of these reception centres; and it was announced from Geneva that there would be full and close co-operation between the United Nations Commission for Refugees and the Pakistan Government in arranging for the return and the rehabilitation of East Pakistanis returning from West Bengal. Next month, a representative of the High Commissioner was stationed in Dacca to coordinate the work. His office was designated by the Secretary-General of the United Nations as the centre for the distribution of the assistance in cash and kind which a number of countries had begun to provide to help in the task of rehabilitation. Shortly before this, a special United Nations envoy, Mr. Kittani, had visited East Pakistan to assess the food needs of the Province; he reported that there was enough food for at least two months more, but that the real problem – as the Government had already found – was to get it where it was wanted. Full agreement had been reached with the authorities on ways of ensuring that aid was distributed only to those for whom it was intended – a precaution to undercut Indian allegations that foreign aid was being either (a) stolen by the Army or (b) used as a 'political weapon' to 'attract "dupes" away from "Bangla Desh".' These preparations for the reception and rehabilitation of returning refugees were again underlined by further announcements of amnesty for all classes except those actually guilty of committing crimes – announcements made in detail both by the President himself and by Lt.-General Tikka Khan as Governor of East Pakistan.

The President appointed a distinguished East Pakistani as Special Adviser to ensure that the Central Government gave the maximum possible help in the process of facilitating the return of the refugees. The result of all this was that from May and June onwards, there was a steady flow both of ordinary people, and of members of the East Bengal Regiment and the East Pakistan Rifles across the frontier. Some of them went to the reception centres, where they received all appropriate help and assistance; others went direct to their homes. Unfortunately, things were made very difficult for those who wished to re-enter East Pakistan. Quite apart from the discouragement naturally resulting from the general atmosphere of tension along the border, from Indian threats of imminent hostilities, and from the shelling and mortaring of villages inside the Pakistan frontier, the Indian authorities deliberately obstructed those refugees who were sufficiently stouthearted, and sufficiently discontented with camp conditions to take the decision to return. All the normal routes were closed, people who tried to use them were turned back, and in certain cases put under arrest. The consequence was that returning refugees were obliged to use byways, and to sneak across the frontier as and when they were able to evade Indian attempts to stop them. As might be expected, the mood of most of them was neither grateful nor charitable towards India; they gave harrowing accounts of how their possessions had been looted from them when they originally arrived in India and how disappointed they had become at their treatment. Plainly it did not suit Indian interests to allow a general return of the refugees until East Pakistan had been turned into 'Bangla Desh'. The Pakistan Government made repeated efforts to relieve India of a burden which she had always claimed to be too heavy to be borne for very long without the world's assistance; Islamabad offered to send reliable officials to the refugee camps to obtain lists of those who wanted to return, and communicate the

had come, in order to ensure that repatriation would be made easy
names to the authorities in the localities from which the refugees
for all concerned. Delhi refused. The United Nations offered to send
impartial observers to both sides of the frontier so that the refugees
could be satisfied that it would be entirely safe for them to return.
Pakistan eagerly accepted the plan; again Delhi refused, while at the
same time redoubling efforts to aggravate border tension and to
hinder by sabotage and terrorism the restoration of ordered conditions in East Pakistan. The outside world was repeatedly told of
the high state of efficiency which had now been attained by the
'freedom fighters' (operating, of course, from the haven of Indian
territory) of their admirable morale, and of their patriotic determination to 'free Bangla Desh' from the oppression of the militarists.

In point of fact, when my wife and I visited East Pakistan in July
1971 – our visit coincided with that of Tunku Abdurrahman, Secretary-General of the newly-formed world organization of Muslim
Countries, who was favourably impressed by the arrangements made
for the reception of the returning refugees – we found that the
prevailing mood of ordinary people was that of relief that the
anarchy caused by the tactics of the Awami League had come to an
end. Peace committees were being formed in all the larger towns,
extending downwards to Union, Tahsil and Sub-Divisional levels, to
reassure citizens that it was now safe for them to go about their
ordinary business. Communications by post and telegraph had been
restored throughout the Province; the damage still being caused by
saboteurs to roads and bridges was more of a nuisance than a danger,
as was the occasional interruption of public utilities such as electri-
city, gas, power and hydroplants. Now that people were free to speak
their minds without fear of the Awami League strong-arm squads, it
was possible to form some impression of the prevailing mood. We
found a few people who resented the action of the Army – mainly, I
think, because they thought it represented the interests of West
Pakistan – but even they believed that Sheikh Mujibur Rahman had
gone too far when he aimed at setting up an independent State. On
the other hand, the Sheikh was still greatly respected as a champion
of the rights of East Pakistan – his propaganda about 'exploitation'
by West Pakistan had obviously bitten quite deeply – and many
people thought that his Six Points were on the right lines to secure
East Pakistan's proper position in the new constitution. Many former
adherents of the Awami League told us that they would not have

voted as they did had they known that Sheikh Mujibur Rahman would alter his programme by substituting the idea of secession for that of securing the maximum autonomy for East Pakistan within a democratic constitution for Pakistan as a whole. Everyone to whom we talked was eager to make a start on democratic institutions, and we were told by some very respected political leaders that they foresaw no difficulty in the President's plan of filling through by-elections the seats in the National and Provincial Assemblies made vacant by people who had run away to India. We encountered a good deal of local annoyance in University centres like Dacca and Rajshahi at Western gullibility in believing absurd inventions like the alleged massacres of staff and students, which never happened at all; formal statements were drawn up by well-known Faculty members contradicting these inventions in detail. A number of Hindu Professors and Lecturers who had sought refuge in Calcutta to avoid the disturbances had by this time returned to Dacca to resume their duties. There was strong feeling against India for what was regarded as her interference in Pakistan's affairs and this feeling was particularly strong among foreign business men, who were receiving clandestine messages from former employees now in India – such as labourers in the Sylhet tea-gardens – that they were only too anxious to return to resume their work, but that the Indian authorities would not allow them to come back.

By the time that the autumn of 1971 was reached, President Yahya Khan was able to publish a list of National and Provincial Assembly members who had forfeited their seats and whose places would be filled by by-elections, the dates of which were also announced. As a further sign of the general approach to normal conditions in East Pakistan, the President appointed his Special Adviser on Refugees, Dr. A. M. Malik, to be civil Governor of the Province. Dr. Malik is an administrator of great experience who has been associated with the government of Pakistan since early days. He served in the Cabinet of Liaquat Ali Khan, the country's first Prime Minister, as Minister for Minority Affairs. More recently, he was President Yahya Khan's Minister for Health, Labour, Works and Social Welfare until the Cabinet was dissolved in February 1971 in preparation for the handing over of power which the President hoped at that time would be achieved in the very near future. Dr. Malik was invited to name his Council of Ministers and present the list for the usual approval. The President also issued a further and even more comprehensive amnesty to encourage the refugees to return. In addition, duly elected members of the National and Provincial Assemblies against whom no charges had been made, but who had gone to India to escape the disturbances, were assured that no cognisance would be taken of their action in crossing the border.

Towards the end of August Mr. Sultan Mohammad Khan, Pakistan's Foreign Secretary, while attending meetings of his country's foreign envoys in Teheran and Geneva, reported to the United Nations High Commissioner for Refugees in Geneva on the steps which the Pakistan Government were taking to facilitate the return and rehabilitation of displaced persons. But he pointed out that his Government's unilateral action could not produce the desired results unless India co-operated. The High Commissioner's representative in East Pakistan, Mr. Kelley, had already toured extensively on the border and had made an assessment of the supporting staff required. During the same month, Pakistan made another effort to secure a reduction of the border tension which was among the main obstacles to the return of the refugees by suggesting to the President of the Security Council that the Council should appoint a Good Offices Committee from among its members to visit the areas of tension and procure some easement of the situation. The letter conveying the suggestion pointed out that so long as India trained, organized, financed and directed forces attempting to procure the dismemberment of Pakistan and to inflict grave damage on East Pakistan's economy, the refugees could not be expected to return to their homes and the human tragedy would continue to deepen.

Contrary to the allegations put forward by 'Bangla Desh' supporters and their friends abroad, the men and women in East Pakistan who are now joining together to rebuild political and economic life in that Province after the ruin brought about by the Awami League rebellion are not 'stooges' but include some of the most respected figures in public life. Some of them were firm supporters of the Awami League in its programme of maximum local autonomy; they only left it when it changed the demand for maximum local autonomy into a bid for secession. It is the firm impression of the present writer that if only India will leave East Pakistan to settle her own affairs and will refrain from giving countenance and active assistance to disruptive elements, East Pakistan is entirely capable of working a democratic form of constitution which will ensure to her full rights and an adequate share in the ordering of the affairs of the Pakistani nation. As a further indication of the gradual return to normal conditions, foreign journalists were again admitted to East Pakistan in the course of the summer, although a disastrously heavy monsoon made it difficult for them to travel widely. This was not the fault of the authorities, local and central, who gave them all the facilities that were possible. But it must be added that such factual reports as they sent arrived in the western world too late to alter the balance of opinion as between Pakistan and India; Indian views of the situation in East Pakistan had remained for so long almost unchallenged that they had become accepted as facts rather than as interested and partisan statements propounding only one side of the case.

While this book was in the Press, two further developments occurred. During the sessions of the United Nations Assembly, it became clear that Pakistan had won substantial support for her contention that the troubles in the Eastern Wing were a domestic matter for which she was seeking an essentially political solution, and that outside interference with this process was neither necessary nor desirable. Secondly, President Yahya Khan lifted the ban on political activity which had been imposed after the Awami League rebellion, subject only to regulations forbidding political pressure on schools, colleges and newspapers, as well as propaganda directed against the integrity of Pakistan. Polling for the 78 National Assembly seats rendered vacant by disqualification – the seats of Sheikh Mujibur Rahman and of Dr. Kamal Hussein were not among those so listed – was fixed for December 1971. It was thus made clear that President Yahya Khan, in spite of the many difficulties which he had encountered, had not been deflected from his long-standing aim of transferring power to popularly-elected members of the National Assembly and of the Provincial Assemblies operating a Constitution based upon a slightly-modified Legal Framework Order of the scope earlier described.

Chapter 7 After the Rebellion: Economic Reconstruction

SOURCES *Report of the National Economic Council (Press Summary)*
Press Conference of Mr.M.M.Ahmad, Economic Adviser
to the President, introducing the National Budget
for fiscal year 1971–72
Report of United Nations Assistant Secretary-General
for Inter-Agency Affairs

The return and resettlement of the refugees figured high among the problems which the Central and the Provincial Government faced in East Pakistan during the summer and autumn of 1971, but it had to be viewed against the background of a deeply disturbed economy. As was pointed out by Mr. Kitani, the United Nations Assistant Secretary-General of Inter-Agency Affairs, in a detailed report released in July, the people of East Pakistan had been afflicted with a major cyclone, with floods, and with civil disturbances, all within the space of six months. In order to cope with the needs of returning refugees and of other persons affected by these disturbances, grants for house-building, clothing, cash doles and vocational rehabilitation amounting to $40m. were needed, besides blankets, tents and corrugated iron sheets. On the food side, the needs of free distribution in the distressed areas were, he estimated, 250,000 tons in addition to the balance of 200,000 tons due under the cyclone disaster relief fund and 100,000 tons of edible oil. In store at Chittagong there were 200,000 tons of food grains, while about 37,500 tons had already been sent inland in June. To ensure the rapid distribution of food, the Pakistan Government needed 15 coaster vessels, 15 lighter vessels for river use, ten tugs and 1,000 five-ton trucks for road transport. Mr. Kitani estimated that shipments of food grains already scheduled to reach Pakistan up to the end of August amounted to 450,000 tons. As a result of this report, which warmly commended the efforts which the Pakistan authorities were already making to deal with the situation, the Secretary-General of the United Nations launched an appeal for a fund of $28m. The initial results were disappointing. By September 1971 only $4m. had come in, Britain being the largest contributor with a gift of £1m. At the end of July, Pakistan was still waiting for the aid that she needed. President Yahya Khan told Press and Television correspondents on July 30 that out of the 30 odd vessels needed to move food inland, only three had so far arrived – a gift from China.

The result was that Pakistan was obliged to make heavy calls upon her own national maritime resources for the relief of East Pakistan. The National Shipping Corporation, which owns 32 seagoing vessels, co-operated closely with the East Pakistan Shipping Corporation in providing the tonnage necessary for the transport of foodstuffs. As the Director of a British-based shipping line pointed out in a letter to *The Times*, there is normally a heavy monthly flow of shipments of wheat and rice, arranged and paid for by the Central Government from Karachi to East Pakistan. Further, rice steadily flows in from Burma, Japan and China – which last country also sends vital supplies of coal. This same gentleman, whose firm is closely connected with shipments to and from Pakistan, stated from his own observation that since the East Pakistan tragedy there had been an enormous increase in the fixing of ships for the transport of wheat and rice from Karachi to Chittagong and Chalna, amounting to hundreds of thousands of tons even in the two months immediately preceding his letter, which was dated at the beginning of September. In addition, there had been heavy shipments of food grains from the USA to Chalna and Chittagong under the American PL 480 programme. His latest information from his East Pakistani shipping associates was that vessels were turning round quicker in Chittagong than they had done for a long time, and that this port, as well as Chalna, was working extremely well. He further pointed out that this quick turn-round argued an efficient system of bulk unloading; and that thanks to American aid, the Pakistan Government had been able to purchase, from all over the world, shallow draft vessels to run up and down the waterways, and carry foodstuffs to many of the places in which it was needed. He concluded by saying that he had no reason to support the Pakistan Government, but he thought it was time someone was allowed to say what was being done by the Western wing to help East Pakistan out of its difficulties.

It is worth noting, in passing, that quite apart from the special efforts which the Pakistan Government were making to deal with the emergency, the nature of this extensive inter-Wing trade completely disposes of the allegation that East Pakistan has been 'exploited like a colonial possession'. A study of the Trade figures –

the latest statistics of which were published in June 1971 – shows that the two Wings have for some time been selling to each other manufactured goods of approximately equal value. In fact, in many years, East Pakistan has a slight edge in this field. Where West Pakistan tends to export more than she imports is in respect of food grains, raw cotton and oilseeds, in the production of which East Pakistan is deficient. West Pakistan does not manufacture East Pakistan's raw jute, but East Pakistan does manufacture West Pakistan's raw cotton. Moreover, the betel nut, spices, timber, fruit, vegetables and pulses which East Pakistan exports to West Pakistan provide no raw materials for West Pakistan's manufacturing industries. Thus the element of 'colonial type exploitation' which strictly means extracting cheap raw materials and selling them back to the vendors after manufacture at a high profit has no application at all to the inter-wing trade of Pakistan. The economies of the two wings are almost entirely complementary, whatever may be alleged to the contrary.

This is not to say that the two economies are equally diversified or equally advanced. A comparison of *per capita* incomes shows that the figure for East Pakistan is Rs.460. This is higher than the figures for the North-West Frontier Province (Rs.360) and for Baluchistan (Rs.455) but substantially lower than those for Sind with Karachi (Rs.854) and the Punjab (Rs.614). It has long been the aim of the Central Government to correct these disparities, especially during the last decade; figures show that the Central Government's assistance to East Pakistan in the shape of revenue assignments increased from 38% in 1960-61 to 50% in 1968-69. East Pakistanis share of development assistance over the same period rose from 38% to 55%. Against the figures must be set the fact that East Pakistan's contribution to the total realization of Central taxes has always been very low in proportion to the size of her population; between 1960-61 and 1968-69, when her share both in revenue assignments and development loans was rising considerably, her contribution rose only from 26.1% to 26.3%. To put the matter in another way; in 1960-1, East Pakistan received Rs.300m. in development loans as against West Pakistan's Rs.340m; but by 1965-66 East Pakistan was getting Rs.370m. as against West Pakistan's 150m. In 1968-69 East Pakistan's share of development loans was Rs.1060m. while West Pakistan received Rs.780m. In 1969-70 development loans for East Pakistan reached the figure of Rs.1290m; for West Pakistan they were Rs.910m. The same story is told by the details of export credits; between 1965-66 and 1969-70, to take the latest figures, East Pakistan received $.210m. as against West Pakistan's $.192m.

But all these efforts by the Central Government have not so far achieved the aim of substantially reducing the disparity in *per capita* income, already pointed out, between the West and the East Wings. Some of the reasons for this, notably the necessity of creating the infrastructure of business expertise, capital accumulation, and industrial enterprise before any real progress could be made, have been outlined in earlier pages. The difference between East Pakistan, which prior to 1947 was treated as a mere hinterland of Calcutta, lacked opportunities for development, and thus seriously lagged behind other parts of Bengal in economic progress, and West Pakistan, already beginning to show a diversified economy, is illustrated by the fact that while the Gross Provincial Product of East Pakistan achieved the not-discreditable increase of 22% between 1964-65 and 1969-70, West Pakistan showed an increase of 35%. An annual growth-rate of 4.1%, which East Pakistan has attained is something that a good many other parts of the world might envy; but East Pakistanis tend rather to look with a jealous eye on the West Wing's growth figure of 6.1% without realising the very serious nature of the handicaps under which their Province laboured when Pakistan came into being.

Although these handicaps are being gradually overcome, thanks to the persistence of the Central Government, the economy of East Pakistan has remained very vulnerable. The terrible cyclone disaster at the end of 1970 put it under enormous strain and taxed to the uttermost the resources of the Central and Provincial Governments in spite of the assistance which came from other countries. Not only did many hundreds of people perish; many thousands of others were reduced to destitution. Seed stocks were swept away; draught cattle were drowned; cultivation ceased; the winter crop was largely lost. Long before this damage could be made good, the whole economic life of East Pakistan was disrupted by the horrible and unnecessary rebellion launched by the Awami League. Communications were disrupted; orderly existence ceased; industrial enterprises, large and small, were brought to a standstill; the two main ports of Chittagong and Chalna were gravely damaged and their future handling-capacity jeopardized; river craft were burned and sunk; the people whose hard work and business enterprise lay behind all the advances which

East Pakistan had achieved in the economic sphere became the first targets of mob violence. By the time that the Army had restored order, the damage was frightful and millions would have starved to death had it not been for the food imported from West Pakistan and America. The distribution even of this was obstructed to the best of their ability of the 'freedom fighters' – whose misguided efforts enjoyed the active support of India and the encouragement, from a distance, of well-meaning people in Western countries who knew nothing about local conditions. This, in short, was the kind of mess which the Central Government of Pakistan and the Provincial Government of East Pakistan were called upon to clear up. In their task they received valuable help from abroad but also a great deal of misconceived criticism. But foreigners who were in a position to see for themselves what the Government was doing took a less biased view. In the third week of August 1971 Mr. Maurice J. Williams, Deputy Administrator for the U S Agency for International Development, who was visiting Pakistan in connection with the generous American aid programme, declared that he was 'very much impressed with the all-out priority the Pakistan Government is placing on relief work in the East Wing'. The main American contribution has been the supply of food under the P L 480 programme; but this was backed up by charters for ships to carry food from ports to inland areas. At the time of Mr. Williams' visit, three coasters had already arrived; 13 more were due before the end of August and 10 were scheduled to come in September. This no doubt allayed some of the anxieties about the shortage of inland shipping which President Yahya Khan had expressed at the end of July; and the Pakistan authorities were further heartened by a promise of all-out American help in their efforts to stimulate economic activity in the East Wing.

When order was restored, it became possible to assess in detail the damage which had been inflicted upon East Pakistan's economy by the disorders of March and April 1971. The large mills and other projects financed by the Pakistan Industrial Credit and Investment Corporation had suffered less than smaller businesses in plant, machinery and buildings; labour attendance soon improved, and before long normal production was resumed. Unsold stocks had led to shortage of working capital, the P I C I C not only arranged to supply this, but also sanctioned loans in foreign currency equivalent to £4.8m. for five new projects, three for weaving broad loom cloth for export, and two for spinning blended yarn, also mainly for export. Further, under the leadership of the State Bank, a banking consortium was set up to provide financial assistance for revitalizing and restoring transport, for new projects proposed by the East Pakistan Industrial Corporation, and for the expansion of the work of the East Pakistan Small Industries Corporation. The needs of the Tea Board, the Port Trust, the Railways and the Inland Waterways Transport Authority were also taken into account. The initial instalment of this financial assistance amounted to Rs.200m., towards which each Bank contributed on an agreed basis, the State Bank arranging re-finance in light of the overall position. The Banks were given credit targets for the ensuing six months, and to encourage them to achieve these targets and to ensure reasonable interest rates, the State Bank offered an interest subsidy on the increase of their lendings, excluding loans to Government and public sector agencies. It was laid down that at least one-fourth of the additional credits must be by way of small loans.

One of the most urgent tasks was to get the jute industry going again. The main problem here was not so much credit – although the banking consortium agreed to provide what was wanted – as to get cash to the growers and to get the crop to the mills. The consortium arranged to open booths in primary jute centres and other jute areas where banking facilities are not available. By these and other measures the traditional pattern of the jute industry was gradually restored in spite of the difficulties arising from the disruption of the communications and the activities of the 'freedom fighters', so that before long the mills in Dacca and Narayanganj were working double shifts.

But while this process of recreating East Pakistan's economic structure was in full swing, another natural catastrophe struck that ill-starred Province. Fresh floods caused by rivers in spate affected seven districts – Faridpur, Rajshahi, Pabna, Jessore, Comilla and Dacca, damaging a million acres of standing crops over an area of about 4000 square miles. The number of people thus rendered homeless and destitute was reckoned at something like 4.5m. Similar floods, potentially almost as serious struck parts of West Pakistan, but the dense population of the East Wing made the damage in that part of the country more extensive and more difficult to repair. The President at once sanctioned Rs.2.5m. from his special relief fund to help the East Pakistan authorities cope with the situation. The work was undertaken with great energy; seven main zones and thirty-seven sub-zones were manned to organize relief work from ninety-seven local centres in Kushtia District alone. A similar pattern was followed in other places. In contrast to the effects of the great cyclone, the loss of life in the August floods was comparatively small – early figures put it at under 100. But the economic loss was savage, and it introduced a new and formidable complication into the problem of providing – and distributing – the food which East Pakistan would need in the months which followed. The trouble in the area devastated by the cyclone was bad enough – cultivation had scarcely begun again owing to the loss of draught cattle and other facilities, although a British team representing Christian Aid, Oxfam, and War on Want had begun operations with tractors – but, in addition, here was an entirely fresh area, where the crops had been quite promising, which had to be struck off as a source of food and at the same time had added a substantial quota to the millions of people already destitute. Representatives of British charitable organizations who visited Pakistan to assess the probable needs of these people during the late autumn and winter of 1971 expressed themselves forcibly on the poor response to the United Nations appeal set on foot by the Secretary-General, frankly admitting at the same time, that the necessary relief work, no matter where the funds came from, would have to rely heavily upon the co-operation of the Pakistan Army. As has already been mentioned on a previous page, the sterling work which the Armed Forces carried through after the cyclone disaster has never been recognized because of the misrepresentation deliberately fostered by the Awami League. It is perhaps significant that reliance should now be placed on that same Army as an essential element in relief work by impartial foreign observers.

The assistance which has come from external sources has already been most valuable to the Central and Provincial Governments in their efforts to rebuild the damaged economy of East Pakistan; but in the last resort it is these Governments which must be the main agencies in carrying through this task. Their success is closely bound up with the strength of the economy of Pakistan as a whole. Although in April the Government requested a moratorium of six months in foreign debt repayments, the prudent financial management of past years had built up a good deal of basic strength. Foreign exchange reserves, which had fallen until February 1971 in the course of the past fiscal year picked up again; and although East Pakistan's exports, because of natural disasters and disturbed conditions, declined by an estimated 23%, this was offset by a remarkable growth of 24% in the exports from West Pakistan. It was not a good year in West Pakistan because of drought and shortage of water in the canals, so that production of major agricultural crops declined slightly; and the national figures, of course, suffered from the setbacks in East Pakistan. But agriculture has made great strides as a result of the three last Five-Year Plans; and as the President pointed out in his survey of June 28, 1971, the country is now, in normal times, on the threshold of self-sufficiency in food. The large inter-Wing trade which supplies East Pakistan from West Pakistan has already been mentioned; even so, overall agricultural production was about 3.5% lower than in the previous year. The rate of increase in industrial production, probably owing to the political uncertainties and stresses of the election year, was just under 3% as compared with 8.8% in 1969-70.

The Pakistan Government faced up to the overall situation with courage, and produced an austerity Budget with a special additional allocation to repair the damage to East Pakistan's economy. This amounted to Rs.2790m., including Rs.300m. for flood control; Rs.100m. for reconstruction in the cyclone-affected areas. A further Rs.150m. was provided for restoring and improving transport facilities damaged during the disturbances. Preferential credit facilities, tax deferments, and funds for providing an additional 20,000 tube wells for winter irrigation in East Pakistan again illustrated the determination of the Central Government to ensure that the needs of the East Wing were given due priority. The keynote of the whole Budget was national self-reliance; its intention was to lay the main burdens of taxation upon the shoulders which could best bear them, and to safeguard the interests of the common man. East Pakistan's needs are greatest; therefore East Pakistan has to have the major slice of the national cake – regardless of the fact that it is her own economic shortfall which has made that cake smaller than usual.

This, surely, is the kind of attitude which should characterize the Government of a country pledged to carry into practice the ideals which inspired its Founder, Quaid-i-Azam Mohammed Ali Jinnah. So long as the Government of Pakistan feel that they are doing their best to live up to those ideals, they are unlikely to be deflected from their course by outside opinion. They are grateful for the support which they are receiving from many countries which understand what they are trying to do, in the face of so many difficulties, some of which are certainly not of their own making; but they are naturally saddened to find that other countries, to which they confidently looked for similar understanding, have been misled by clever and interested misrepresentations of their aims and actions.

Appendix 1 Sources for further study of the Economic Relations between East and West Pakistan

As mentioned earlier on in this book, there has been much misrepresentation of the economic relationship between East and West Pakistan. Quite responsible people who are ignorant of the facts, repeat charges of 'colonial type' exploitation against the Central Government.

All the relevant statistics are available to those who take the trouble to look them up; but until a short time ago, they were dispersed among a number of the publications of the Central Office of Statistics.

In June and July, 1971, however, the figures specifically relating to the details of inter-Wing economic relationships were gathered together in two handy and compact brochures, which provide statistical evidence for the facts set out in Chapter 7.

The first, entitled *Economic Development in East Pakistan; Role of the Central Government,* sets out in detail what has been done to bring East Pakistan forward economically since 1947.

The second, published in July 1971, entitled *East Pakistan's Share in Central Revenue and Expenditure* shows in tabular form how East Pakistan has fared in the distribution of Public Sector outlays, Development Loans, Financial Assistance to Provinces, Grants, Loans, Export Credits, Regional Distribution of International and Inter-Wing Trade, Private Investment, Fiscal Concessions, and the like. The striking fact emerges that while East Pakistan's contribution to Central taxes amounts only to 26.3% of the total, the Province receives as Revenue Assignment 50% of the total.

The brochure on *Economic Development in East Pakistan; Role of the Central Government* also sets out facts which run contrary to widely-accepted – but quite erroneous – assertions circulated for purely political purposes. East Pakistan, since 1958-9 has overtaken and surpassed West Pakistan in Grants-in-Aid, in its share of Central Taxes and Duties and in Public Sector expenditure. Taking the total development programme, public and private, which rose from Rs.1260m in 1960-61 to Rs.3762.4m in 1969-70, and is estimated at Rs.5280m in 1970-71, for East Pakistan, the increase is about 199%, and has been particularly fast during the Second and Third Plan periods.

As I have already stated there is now a constitutional obligation to remove disparities in *per capita* incomes between different parts of Pakistan. From this obligation, East Pakistan has already benefited largely in the Third Plan; while the Fourth Plan envisages a growth rate of 7.5% per annum as against West Pakistan's 5.5%. During the last few years, in particular, efforts have been made to channel a larger volume of credit to East Pakistan through the Agricultural Development Bank, the Industrial Development Bank, Pakistan Industrial Credit and Investment Corporation, the House Building Finance Corporation, and similar institutions. Side by side with this, the total allocation of foreign exchange in the private sector alone now stands at 41%.

Appendix **2**   The Awami League's Six Points

(Extract from Awami League Manifesto)

Pakistan shall be a Federation granting
full autonomy on the basis of the six-point formula
to each of the federating units:

POINT no 1   The character of the Government shall be federal and parliamentary, in which the election to the Federal Legislature and to the legislature of the federating units shall be direct and on the basis of universal adult franchise. The representation in the federal legislature shall be on the basis of population.

POINT no 2   The Federal Government shall be responsible only for defence and foreign affairs and subject to the conditions provided in (3) below, currency.

POINT no 3   There shall be two separate currencies mutually or freely convertible in each wing for each region, or in the alternative a single currency, subject to the establishment of a federal reserve system in which there will be regional federal reserve banks which shall devise measures to prevent the transfer of resources and flight of capital from one region to another.

POINT no 4   Fiscal policy shall be the responsibility of the federating units. The federal government shall be provided with requisite revenue resources for meeting the requirements of defence and foreign affairs, which revenue resources would be automatically appropriable by the Federal Government in the manner provided and on the basis of the ratio to be determined by the procedure laid down in the Constitution. Such constitutional provisions would ensure that Federal Government's revenue requirements are met consistently with the objective of ensuring control over the fiscal policy by the Governments of the federating units.

POINT no 5   Constitutional provisions shall be made to enable separate accounts to be maintained of the foreign exchange earnings of each of the federating units, under the control of the respective governments of the federating units. The foreign exchange requirement of the Federal Government shall be met by the Governments of the federating units on the basis of a ratio to be determined in accordance with the procedure laid down in the Constitution. The regional governments shall have power under the constitution to negotiate foreign trade and aid within the framework of the foreign policy of the country, which shall be the responsibility of the Federal Government.

POINT no 6   The Government of the federating units shall be empowered to maintain a militia or para-military force in order to contribute effectively towards national security.

Appendix 3   The Legal Framework Order of 1970

This order was drawn up to provide a basis for the elections, for the creation of the National and Provincial Assemblies, and for the drafting of a Constitution of democratic Parliamentary type. It represented the maximum measure of agreement which the President had been able to find in his conferences with political leaders along the following lines:

Pakistan to be a Federal Islamic Republic, with free and periodical elections based on adult suffrage for the National and Provincial Assemblies on the basis of population; fundamental rights for citizens to be laid down and guaranteed; independent judiciary to dispense justice and enforce fundamental rights; maximum devolution of powers legislative administrative and financial compatible with a Federal Centre adequate to discharge its responsibilities in external and internal affairs and in preserving the independence and territorial integrity of Pakistan; guarantee of minority rights.

The National Assembly was to be the first legislature of the nation, if unicameral, and the Lower House if the constitution was to be bicameral; but this was not to happen until the National Assembly had completed within 120 days its primary task, that of framing the constitution, and the constitution had been ratified by the President.

Membership of the National Assembly was to total 313; East Pakistan to have 162 members and 7 women members; The Punjab was to have 82 members and 3 women members: Sind to have 27 members and 1 woman member; Baluchistan was to have 4 members and 1 woman member; the North West Frontier Province was to have 18 members and no specified number of women; the Centrally-administered Tribal Area was given 7 members and 1 woman. There was nothing to prevent women being elected from general constituencies. For the Provincial Assemblies, that of East Pakistan was to number 300 with 10 women members; the Punjab 180 with 6 women members; Sind, 60 with 2 women members; Baluchistan, 20, with 1 woman member; North-West Frontier Province 40, with 2 women members.

The remainder of the Framework Order laid down rules for the election of the Speaker and Deputy Speaker, for the transaction of business, for bringing motions and so forth. It was a most useful guide to current parliamentary practice as known in western parliaments, and unexceptionable in its contents. But the National Assembly was charged with the responsibility of settling its own voting rules for the framing of the Constitution, which, as the President insisted more than once in his speeches, was not an ordinary piece of legislation, but 'an agreement to live together'. After the original failure of the National Assembly to meet in the spring of 1971, modifications were introduced into the Legal Framework Order relieving the Assembly of the responsibility of framing a constitution, but conferring powers to amend the constitution which would be submitted to it. The National Assembly was to become the National Legislature at once, instead of being a Constituent Asembly also.

The full text of the Legal Framework Order is to be found on pp. 18–35 of the August 1971 White Paper on the Crisis in East Pakistan.

Appendix **4**   Hijacking of Indian plane to Lahore
Findings of judicial enquiry commission released

Islamabad, April 20

A Commission of Inquiry was appointed in March this year by the President to enquire into the circumstances of the hijacking of an Indian civil aircraft to Lahore on January 30, 1971, to find out the persons responsible for it and to determine the motives behind the incident. The Commission headed by Mr. Justice Noorul Arfin, Judge of the High Court of Sind and Baluchistan, submitted its report to the President on April 15, 1971.

The Commission examined a number of witnesses besides the two hijackers, Mohammad Hashim Qureshi and Mohammad Ashraf Qureshi.

According to a summary of the report released here today, the Commission has come to the conclusion that Pakistan was in no way responsible for, nor in any way connected with, the hijacking incident. In fact, the Commission pointed out, that as soon as the hijacked aircraft landed at Lahore airport, the Governmental authorities in Pakistan took every step to protect members of the crew, the passengers and the aircraft. They extended every co-operation and facility to the Indian High Commission in Pakistan to remain in contact with the passengers and members of the crew, who were safely taken to and allowed to cross the border into India. The authorities in Pakistan took all possible steps to protect the Indian plane. Immediate possession of the aircraft was not possible for two reasons. One, because the hijackers were reported to be armed with a revolver and a hand-grenade, which were found to be dummy weapons only after the destruction of the aircraft. And, two, as the news of the hijacked aircraft spread, large crowds collected at the airport creating a serious law and order situation. Despite this, the Governmental authorities took steps on February 2 to isolate the hijackers so that conditions could be created for taking possession of the aircraft. But as soon as the hijackers realized that these steps were afoot and that the aircraft may be released to India they destroyed it by setting fire to it. Their action was promptly deplored by the Government of Pakistan.

From the evidence produced before it, the Commission has come to the conclusion that the hijacking of the aircraft was arranged by the Indian Intelligence Agencies as the culmination of a series of actions taken by the Indian Government to bring about a situation of confrontation between Pakistan and India. These included Indian attacks on Batrigachh, and other Pakistani enclaves in December 1970, externment of Sheikh Abdullah and Mirza Afzal Beg, banning of Plebiscite Front and expulsion of a First Secretary of Pakistan High Commission in New Delhi.

The Commission says that the hijacking incident occurred at a time when talks were in progress between the leaders of the Awami League and the Pakistan People's Party for the resolution of the differences arising from their programmes. Subsequent events like arms aid by India to subversive elements in East Pakistan and the concentration of the Indian forces on the East Pakistan border have led the Commission to take the view that another additional motive behind this incident was to disrupt communications within Pakistan and to dislocate movement of people and supplies between the two wings and thereby to create a state of tension between the various regions of Pakistan with a view to strengthening separatist tendencies. This object was sought to be achieved by the sudden imposition of ban with effect from February 4, 1971, on flights of Pakistani aircraft over Indian territory, particularly the territory between East Pakistan and West Pakistan. Another motive behind the incident would appear to be a desire to weaken Pakistan financially.

Dealing with the circumstances of hijacking, the Commission says on January 28, 1971, Ashraf booked two seats by air journey from Srinagar to Jammu, one in his own name and the other for Hashim but in the name of Mohammad Husain. They left their homes for Srinagar airport in the morning of January 30, 1971, but on the way they were checked by a military post. When they reached the airport there were at least three members of the Indian Intelligence/Security Services at the airport, all of whom knew Hashim. One was Dawarka Nath, Inspector of the Indian-held Kashmir CID, the other was Chabeel Singh, Havildar in BSF and the third was a member of the Indian Intelligence, who was standing near the aircraft, later hijacked. Dawarka Nath insisted that Hashim should entertain him to tea and when Hashim pleaded that he had no money, Dawarka Nath put his hand into Hashim's overcoat pocket, from where he took out a cyclostyled poster in Urdu, entitled 'Jehad has begun'. This fact is mentioned in the Hindu, Madras of February 11, 1971. However, they boarded the plane without any hindrance and the aircraft duly took off for Jammu. When the announcement was made that the aircraft was about to land at Jammu airport both Hashim and Ashraf stood up. Hashim ran into the cockpit where he put a dummy revolver on the left side of the neck of the pilot and informed him that he and Ashraf were N L F workers and were hijacking the aircraft to Pakistan. Ashraf took his post at the door between the cockpit and passengers, cabin with the dummy hand-grenade in his hand and informed passengers and other members of the crew to remain seated quietly as otherwise he would blow up the aircraft with the hand-grenade. The pilot contacted the Airport Control Tower at Lahore and entered into Pakistan.

The report says that the circumstances under which Hashim and Ashraf left the Srinagar airport on January 30 strengthens the Commission in its view that hijacking of the Indian aircraft was not an act of freedom fighters but was carried out with the blessings and complicity of the Indian authorities. It should be noted that the hijackers carried a dummy revolver and a dummy hand-grenade. The question is why, with Hashim Qureshi's connection with the B S F and the Indian Intelligence Service, it was not possible for him to obtain a real revolver. The idea cannot be ruled out that the persons who planned the hijacking of the aircraft did not wish to expose the members of the crew and the passengers to unnecessary risks. Moreover, the evidence before the Commission is that notwithstanding the fact that Hashim was in the employment of the BSF as well as the Indian Intelligence Bureau, he himself was kept under constant surveillance. In New Delhi, he was always in the company of Inspector Ghulam Husain Mir and in Srinagar he was either in the company of this Mir or in that of Dawarka Nath. He was not allowed to enter Srinagar airport except when he was accompaneid by Dawarka Nath. Still, Hashim and Ashraf were allowed to board the aircraft without any search.

From the fact that Hashim was under constant surveillance it appears inconceivable to the Commission that the Indian authorities were not aware of Hashim's preparations for hijacking and his boarding the aircraft for this purpose. Even the way the aircraft was hijacked indicates that the whole thing had been stage-managed. Hashim put the dummy revolver on the left side of the neck of the pilot but a bare glance would have shown to the co-pilot that it was a toy weapon. Likewise, an experienced military man like Captain Mohan Singh of the Assam Rifles who was sitting just in front of Ashraf in the passenger cabin could surely recognize that Ashraf was not holding a genuine grenade. But no attempt was made to overpower either Hashim or Ashraf. Another aspect of the whole affair which has attracted the notice of the Commission is the behaviour of Hashim after the aeroplane had landed at the airport. Hashim pretended he was not sure that the plane had landed at Lahore or some other place in Pakistan and therefore he made the Civil Aviation officials and personnel of Security and PIA Services at the airport produce evidence to satisfy him that he was really in Pakistan territory. Yet it was stated before the Commission that when the aeroplane entered into Pakistan territory Hashim made the Captain fly it at a low altitude and, in this way, he recognized the GT Road and even the Badshahi mosque of Lahore. It appears that Hashim put on this act to create the impression that he and Ashraf were in fact freedom fighters who, in hijacking the aircraft from Indian-held Kashmir, were moved by patriotic zeal. The Commission is of the view that Hashim knew very well that the aircraft had in fact landed at the Lahore airport.

As to the antecedents of the hijackers, particularly Hashim, the report says the evidence which has come before the Commission shows that Hashim is neither a revolutionary, nor a patriot, nor in any way interested in any liberation or political movement in Indianheld Kashmir.

The report says that Hashim visited Pakistan twice before the hijacking incident. During his first visit on passport which ended on January 26, 1970, he came with other family members to stay with his maternal uncle Ghulam Nabi Baig in Peshawar, where he showed keenness to contact Mr. Maqbool Butt, President of the Plebiscite Front in Azad Kashmir and a member of the Central High Command of NLF, who was already known to Mr. Baig. According to Mr. Maqbool Butt, Hashim asked him to enroll him in NLF. Hashim returned to Indian-held Kashmir on January 26, 1970 and re-entered Pakistan illegally during April 1970. On this occasion he suggested to Maqbool Butt that he could hijack an Indian plane to Pakistan. During this period he was also in correspondence with Maqbool Butt. The Commission has it on record that these letters were seen by the Indian-held Kashmir Police before despatch.

Hashim's conduct would reasonably lead to the conclusion that from the very beginning he was acting as an Indian Intelligence agent.

The report brings out Hashim's contacts with several Indian Intelligence men including Lt.-Col. Ashok Kumar Patel and Mr. Ghulam Hassan Mir, the former being Assistant Director and the latter Inspector of B S F Intelligence and Mr. A. S. Mathur, Deputy Director of Indian Intelligence Bureau, in charge of the Intelligence Sub-Bureau at Srinagar.

The Commission draws attention to Sheikh Abdullah's letter to Mr. Jaya Prakash Narayan, published in the *Indian Express*, New Delhi of February 15, 1971, in which he said:

'The recent unfortunate events in the sub-continent have further exacerbated the already strained relations between the two neighbours. The story, however, does not end with the hijacking and blowing up of the plane. The important question is on whom to fix the responsibility. The revelations made since the incident, by the responsible quarters, have raised grave doubts in my mind and perhaps in the minds of many others, as to the veracity of the stories put out in regard to the agencies responsible for this act. Nevertheless, it has become abundantly clear that the chief hijacker was an employee of the Border Security Force. He had crossed over to Pakistan and reportedly got training in hijacking there; after re-crossing to this side of the cease-fire line, he was re-employed by the Security Force, and stationed on duty at the airport, ostensibly to keep watch on possible hijacking, as reported by the Press. The hijacker had told his employers the possibility of "skyjacking", which information was communicated to the Kashmir Government by the agency under whose employ the hijacker was. The Kashmir Police wanted to interrogate the person, but according to the Chief Minister, Mr. Sadiq, the agency refused to identify him or surrender him to the Kashmir Police for interrogation. Finally, the man with one of his accomplices, boards the plane with the full knowledge of the Border Security Force, and carries out his mission, forcing the plane to land at Lahore. His first act there was to contact a person who is reported to be the leader of the Kashmir Liberation Front, named Mohd. Maqbool Butt. Now this Maqbool Butt was involved in some murder case in Kashmir and was tried and sentenced to death. This happened in 1967 when I was in Kodaikanal and Shri D. P. Dhar, currently Indian Ambassador in Moscow, was in charge of Home Affairs in Kashmir. But before the execution of the sentence, he mysteriously escaped from jail and crossed the border to Pakistan.

'How he managed to escape the jail has up till now remained a mystery. Regarding his enlisting the official assistance in the dramatic escape from the jail, it is being said that he was deliberately allowed to escape and cross over to Pakistan in order to use his services there for furtherance of the plans. The information about the possible hijacking of an Indian plane, had been with the Kashmir Government and Central agencies since July 1969, as reported. But the plan, meaningfully, unfolds itself only after our externment and banning of the Plebiscite Front.'

The Commission also refers to Mr. G. M. Sadiq, Chief Minister of IHK Government's allegation, as reported in the *Hindustan Times,* New Delhi, of February 3, 1971, that Hashim Qureshi was a member of the Border Security Force and that, when the State Police wanted Hashim Qureshi for interrogation, the Central Intelligence Services of India gave him protection and prevented this interrogation being carried out.

Appendix **5**   Lawlessness and violence perpetrated by
the Awami League prior to March 25, 1971

Part 1 DACCA AND ENVIRONS

MARCH 1 Sheikh Mujibur Rahman called a strike in Dacca in protest against the temporary postponement of the meeting of the National Assembly. Awami Leaguers raided the Narayanganj Rifle Club for arms, which were collected by student militants in the Iqbal and Jagannath Halls of Dacca University. From these centres armed gangs collected further arms along with vehicles and forced levies of money. During the night there was widespread looting and extensive damage to property. The troops were confined to barracks.

Sheikh Mujibur Rahman called for a week-long strike throughout East Pakistan.

MARCH 2 Two firearms shops were raided and the arms taken to Dacca University. Practice firing was heard all day on the campus.

Mobs armed with firearms and iron bars raided business premises in Jinnah Avenue and Baitul Mukarram. The Shalimar Hotel and the Gulistan Cinema were attacked and set on fire, as were two private houses in the Farm Gate area. Student groups burned the Pakistan flag. Police Officers reported that their men could not be trusted to restrain mob violence and the Civil authorities asked the help of the military. A curfew was imposed and the troops were called out. An Army truck was attacked at Sadarghat, and in the firing six rioters were killed. Another mob attacked the TV Station and another rioter was killed when the Army fired in defending the Station. There was extensive defiance of the curfew. Arson and looting continued throughout the night.

MARCH 3 Mob violence spread to Islampur, Patuakhali Bazar, Nawabpur and other suburbs of Dacca. Shops, business premises and private houses were looted and set on fire, with the loss of five killed and 62 wounded. Sheikh Mujibur Rahman announced a civil disobedience movement to 'secure the rights of the people of Bangla Desh'. Schools and colleges closed and most of the staff and students of Dacca University dispersed, leaving only a handful of Awami League militants. Radio and TV Stations were compelled to play the new 'Bangla Desh' anthem.

MARCH 4 Looting in Dhanmadi and Nawabpur districts. Another firearms shop raided. (Renewed serious outbreaks at Chittagong and Khulna – see below.)

MARCH 5 Telephone and telegraph employees stopped work on Awami League orders, severing ordinary communications between Dacca and other parts of East Pakistan and between East Pakistan and the outside world including West Pakistan. Militant students attacked British Council offices: troops arrived in time to drive them out.

MARCH 6 Jail break of prisoners from Central Prison. Warders opened fire killing seven. Sergeant and six warders wounded. Prisoners and Awami Leaguers marched in procession through Dacca chanting defiant slogans. Government Science Laboratory attacked and all explosive chemicals and dangerous acids removed. Mobs attacked Polytechnic with similar objectives but troops arrived in time to drive them off.

MARCH 7 Sheikh Mujibur Rahman proclaimed plans for running a parallel government and issued directives for non-payment of taxes; closure of all government offices and courts; closure of all educational institutions; strict adherence of all newspapers, TV and Radio Stations to Awami League directives; ban on bank remittances to West Wing banks; Revolutionary Councils to be set up in each Union, Mohalla, Thana Sub-division and District under leadership of local Awami League units. Explosives thrown into Radio Pakistan building. Student groups seized cars, jeeps, pick-up trucks and micro-buses by force.

MARCH 8 Awami Leaguers, after obtaining official lists of licence-holders, forcibly collected from them all their arms and ammunition. Meetings and processions of a militant character held by armed mobs in many parts of Dacca. Tajuddin Ahmed, General Secretary of the Awami League issued certain clarifications of the previous day's directives, including prohibition of all remittances 'outside Bangla Desh'.

MARCH 9 Check-points set up by Leaguers in various parts of Dacca; belongings of passers-by searched; money confiscated. This process continued over the next few days and was extended to the harassment and intimidation of persons suspected of lukewarm support of the League. Later the Students' Revolutionary Council admitted that many unauthorised persons were raiding private houses and seizing money. Chaos and terorrism throughout Dacca. People trying to leave the city were stopped and molested. Acid thrown at a government office near Kakrail; passengers taken out of trains at the railway station and charged with supporting West Pakistan.

MARCH 14 Sheikh Mujibur Rahman issued fresh directives; one ordered Deputy Commissioners and Sub-divisional Officers to act in cooperation with local Awami League Revolutionary Councils. Customs dues to be credited, not to the Central Government but to two named private banks.

MARCH 15 Taxes to be paid to Awami League Action Committee in Dacca. Action Committees set up throughout East Pakistan in towns and villages to resist the Army should it try to restore governmental authority.

MARCH 17-18 Terrorism, looting and acid-throwing continued. Many private citizens forced to leave their houses because of widespread violence and intimidation. Two acid bottles thrown inside government office in Azimpura, Dacca. The Central Government High School at Motijheel raided and acid and chemicals taken away.

MARCH 19 An Army vehicle on a routine journey from Mymensingh ambushed at a level crossing. All six occupants, along with their weapons, taken away.

MARCH 23 Pakistan Day was celebrated as 'Resistance Day', with parades and marches by para-military 'Liberation Front' troopers and ex-Service men. The Pakistan flag was torn down from buildings and the 'Bangla Desh' flag hoisted. Scuffles broke out between Awami Leaguers and those who resisted this process. At an armed-march-past outside his residence Sheikh Mujibur Rahman took the salute and the "Bangla Desh" flag was ceremonially unfurled. Student groups kidnapped business men and released them only after ransom money had been paid. Outgoing passengers were stoned and mobbed at Dacca Airport.

MARCH 24 Written and cyclostyled posters and leaflets calling the people to arms to resist the troops and bidding them make preparations for house-to-house resistance in the revolutionary struggle were circulated throughout Dacca.

MARCH 25 Extensive manufacture of acid bombs reported in Iqbal and Jagannath Halls of Dacca University; also in the Engineering College. Barricades and road blocks set up in many parts of the city. Sheikh Mujibur Rahman appointed his 'commander-in-chief' along with other high officers.

MARCH 25-26 President Yahya Khan orders the Army to restore governmental authority.

Part 2 OUTSIDE DACCA: JESSORE

MARCH 3 Mob armed with cudgels and spears attacked the Telephone Exchange but were driven off by guards; two killed and nine wounded.

MARCH 4 Deputy Commissioner's office raided; the Pakistan flag torn down and a hand grenade thrown. A train coming from Khulna was derailed and the passengers were pulled out and murdered.

MARCH 6-16 Reign of terror. Many grenades and bombs thrown. The armoury of the Rajendra College O.T.C. was raided; ten rifles and 15 bayonets taken away. The Pakistan flag was burned at Bargana. Awami Leaguers in complete control; 'Bangla Desh' flag flown on all government buildings.

MARCH 17-19 Power house damaged and supply interrupted. Jessore-Khulna road barricaded and blocked at several points. Large supplies of arms from India brought in through Satkhira. Active preparations made to resist the Army if it came.

KHULNA

MARCH 4 The Telephone Exchange was attacked by an armed mob and non-Bengali employees were savagely beaten to death.

MARCH 5 Mobs armed with spears, grenades and cudgels killed 57 non-Bengalis whose mutilated bodies were later found. Four shops looted and a hotel set on fire. Attempts by mobs to loot arms stores were frustrated by the non-Bengali owners, who opened fire killing one and wounding five of the rioters.

MARCH 17 Non-Bengali survivors of the killings of March 5 and who had not been able to flee were again attacked.

MARCH 18 Two acid grenades thrown into local Army camp.

CHITTAGONG

MARCH 1 – onwards. This, the sole deep water port of East Pakistan and the Headquarters of the East Bengal Regiment became a major focus of armed resistance.

MARCH 3-4 Armed mobs attacked the Wireless Colony and the Ferozshah Colony. 700 houses were set on fire and the occupants burned to death. Apart from these victims, whose bodies were found later, over 300 more non-Bengalis were killed or wounded.

MARCH 5 Stabbings of non-Bengalis and burning of their houses continued. Right up to the time when the troops restored order in April, the city was completely under the control of Awami Leaguers. Regular mass-executions of non-Bengalis took place. On March 20, the routine arrival of M.V. Swat, with munitions and supplies for the local garrison became the occasion for mob violence to prevent unloading. Some heavy fighting occurred.

MARCH 25 – APRIL 11 Mass executions, burning and looting continued. Following the projected 'D' day on the night of March 25-26, massive barriers were erected to shut off the port. An estimated 10,000 more non-Bengalis were massacred, including women and children as well as men. Non-Bengali port workers were killed in cold blood. In the Isphani Jute Mills Recreation Club, 152 women and children were slaughtered – their bloodied clothing, and the children's toys mingled with the corpses were found by the Army.

RANGPUR, DINAJPUR, COMILLA, SAIDPUR
MYMENSINGH, BOGRA, RAJSHAHI

In all these places, there was extensive bomb-throwing, looting, arson and murder of non-Bengalis throughout March. The Saidpur Cantonment was fired on. At Santakar, in Bogra District, more than 15,000 non-Bengalis were rounded up and murdered, and their womenfolk paraded naked through the streets. In the Sankipura area of Mymensingh, the men of 2,000 non-Bengali families were taken out and murdered and their womenfolk were compelled to dig their graves. More than 1,500 widows and orphans were sheltered in a mosque by a brave Mullah, who defied the mob calling for their blood. In Rajshahi, the office of the City Magistrate was burned, the 'Bangla Desh' flag hoisted on the Town Hall. Non-Bengali members of the University Staff were saved by the Vice Chancellor and other Bengali Professors who gave a written undertaking that their non-Bengali colleagues would be confined to the University Campus. Thanks to this brave action, no member of the Staff was killed, in spite of threats to the lives of non-Bengalis.

Appendix **6**   The Awami League's Intended Proclamation
Some salient points

The full text of this document is printed on pp. 47–63 of the *White Paper* of August 5.

Its object was to withdraw Martial Law entirely from 'Bangla Desh' from the time when the Governor, to be appointed by the President on the advice of the majority party, took office; and from the rest of Pakistan within seven days of that date. Provisionally, Pakistan was to be governed according to the late constitution as modified by the Proclamation. National Assembly members elected from 'Bangla Desh' were to sit as a Constituent Convention and frame a constitution for 'Bangla Desh' in Dacca; National Assembly members elected from the States of West Pakistan were to sit in Islamabad, to frame a Constitution for the States of West Pakistan. With the exception of carefully restricted powers left to the Central Government, 'Bangla Desh' was to enjoy complete control, not only over domestic affairs but also over taxation, foreign exchange and banking, and was to contribute to Central revenues only to the extent that it agreed. When the constitutions of 'Bangla Desh' and West Pakistan were drafted and agreed, the members elected from 'Bangla Desh' and from West Pakistan States to the National Assembly were to meet for the purpose of framing a Constitution for the 'Confederation of Pakistan'.

If these steps were actually put in practice, the State of Pakistan, as bequeathed by Qaid-i-Azam Mohammad Ali Jinnah would cease to exist.

In drafting this Proclamation, and insisting upon its issue 'within 48 hours' the Awami League and its leaders were:

1   Departing from the provisions of the Legal Framework Order upon which depended the validity of their own election to the National and Provincial Assemblies.

2   Departing from the Six Points which they themselves had prescribed as the basis for any new Constitution.

3   Betraying the confidence of the electors who had returned them on a programme of the Six Points and maximum provincial autonomy consistent with the integrity of Pakistan.

Appendix **7**   Major atrocities committed by
the Awami League after March 25, 1971

(White Paper pp. 64–69)

District	Date (1971) Area	Incident
Chittagong	26-30 MARCH Chittagong Town	The town remained under control of rebel elements of East Bengal Regiment (EBR), East Pakistan Rifles (EPR) and Awami League (AL) volunteers, who went on the rampage looting, massacring and setting fire to entire colonies in the main town as well as in outlying areas. Slaughter houses were set up, including one in the Chittagong office of AL, where men, women and children were systematically massacred. In many cases blood was drained through syringes before bodies were dismembered (10,000 — 12,000 killed).
	27 MARCH Usmania Glass Works	West Pakistani staff tortured and killed. (Casualties 17 killed.)
	19 APRIL Isphahani Jute Mills, and adjoining areas	Women and children brutally murdered. West Pakistani Officers and workers missing/kidnapped. (Casualties: about 1,000.)
	27/28 APRIL Hafiz Jute Mills	Mill premises attacked and a number of employees killed. House of the owner set on fire. All inmates burnt alive except some minor children who escaped. (Casualties believed to be about 150 killed.)

134

District	Date (1971) Area	Incident
	26-30 APRIL Karnaphuli Paper and Rayon Mills, Chandraghona and adjoining areas	Large-scale looting, arson and killing. Women locked up in houses, rescued later, narrated unmentionable stories of rape and brutalities. (Casualties about 2,000 killed.)
	27-30 APRIL Rangamati	West Pakistanis all over Rangamati rounded up, tortured and massacred. (Casualties about 500 killed.)
Jessore	29-30 MARCH Jhumjhumpur Colony	Entire population of Biharis subjected to general massacre by rebel EPR personnel. Women and children dragged towards Narail. About 400-500 women also kidnapped to India by river route. Human skulls and other parts of human body were found lying strewn all over the area. (About 3,000 killed, 2,000 missing.)
	29/30 MARCH Ramnagar Colony	People from Jhumjhumpur Colony took shelter in this colony, which was also set on fire. (Over 150 killed, 448 in destitute camps.)
	30 MARCH Taraganj Colony	AL volunteers and rebel EPR personnel massacred entire colony. Very few survived. All houses destroyed. (About 500 killed, 400 missing.)
	30 MARCH-5 APRIL Hamidpur, Ambagan, Bachachar and Puratan Kasba of Jessore Town	Most of the population of the area was wiped out. Houses were first looted and then destroyed. (About 1,000 killed/missing, 175 in hospital, 172 in destitute camps.)

AL Awami League EBR East Bengal Regiment EPR East Pakistan Rifles

District	Date (1971) Area	Incident
	30 MARCH-5 APRIL Mobarakganj	Men, women and children subjected to torture and killing: their houses looted and set on fire. (Over 200 killed, ten in hospital, 27 in destitute camps.)
	30 MARCH-5 APRIL Kaliganj	Several localities attacked, women raped and men and children killed. Large-scale looting and arson. (About 300 killed, 132 in relief camps.)
	30 MARCH-10 APRIL Kotchandpur	Indiscriminate killing and arson. (About 200 killed, 5 injured, 55 in relief camps.)
	30 MARCH Tasfidanga	Revolutionary Council volunteers attacked a number of houses which were premarked, killed men and old women, and took away younger women. (About 200 killed, 72 in relief camps.)
	30 MARCH- 10 APRIL Narail	Pathans were the main target of atrocities. They were rounded up from all over Narail and brutally done to death. (60-70 Pathans including women and children massacred.)
	25 MARCH- 4 APRIL Jhenidah Sub- Division	AL volunteers attacked a number of houses which were looted and set on fire. Heavy loss of life and property. (More than 250 killed, 50 missing, 10 in hospital.)
Khulna	28/29 MARCH Khulna Town/ Crescent Jute Mills,	AL para-military training camps established in Khulna. Organized murder and arson unleashed

AL Awami League EBR East Bengal Regiment EPR East Pakistan Rifles

District	Date (1971) Area	Incident
	Khalispur and Star Jute Mills, Chandi Mahal	against so-called 'brokers' of West Pakistan. Houses destroyed and large-scale massacre carried out. Before being guillotined, victims were tortured. Innocent women and children were dragged on the road and killed. Survivors found floating in the river were fished out, their stomachs were slit open and then they were again pushed back in the river which ran red with blood. Extensive damage to mill property. Some officers spared on paying ransom. (Casualties: about 5,000 killed.)
	28/29 MARCH People's Jute Mill, Khalispur, Khulna	EPR/Frontier Guards/AL workers indulged in wanton massacre irrespective of their victims' age. (Casualties: 467 killed.)
	28/29 MARCH New Colony, Khalispur, Khulna	Colony surrounded by about 10,000 AL workers. Rebel police also joined in. Firing continued for over six hours. (Casualties: about 300 killed.)
	30 APRIL Satkhira Sub-Division, Khulna	West Pakistan SDO captured and taken prisoner. The area was subjected to mass killing, atrocities and large-scale looting of the town. (Casualties: about 1,000 killed.)
Kushtia	29 MARCH– 10 APRIL Kushtia Town	Rebel EPR/Devotees/local miscreants resorted to indiscriminate firing on Biharis and West Pakistani forces. Reign of terror continued for 13 days. (Casualties: 1,000 to 1,500 killed.)

AL Awami League EBR East Bengal Regiment EPR East Pakistan Rifles

District	Date (1971) Area	Incident
	26 MARCH– 1 APRIL Chuadanga, Kushtia	Biharis and West Pakistanis rounded up and killed. Women subjected to inhuman treatment. West Pakistani SDO mercilessly tortured and his pregnant wife beaten. (Casualties: about 500 killed and 100 missing.)
	23 APRIL Zafar Kandi Kushtia	Bihari colonies were attacked by rebel EPR local miscreants. After large-scale looting of property, the colony was set on fire. No survivors. Women raped and later killed. Their dead bodies were found with breasts cut and wombs slit open. (Casualties: about 500 killed.)
	30 MARCH– 13 APRIL Meherpur, Kushtia	For two weeks, Meherpur was subjected to wanton killings, arson and rape. (Casualties: 400-600 killed, 200 missing, and 10 in hospital.)
Bogra	26 MARCH– 23 APRIL Bogra Town	Jail broken by AL volunteers and prisoners let loose to commit acts of violence and plunder. 7,000 men, women and children huddled into the jail premises which was to be blown up by dynamite but timely arrival of Army rescued them. Eye witnesses narrated stories of mass murders, rape and arson. (About 2,000 reported killed.)

AL Awami League EBR East Bengal Regiment EPR East Pakistan Rifles

District	Date (1971) Area	Incident
	26 MARCH– 22 APRIL Naogaon/Santahar	AL miscreants set up road blocks to prevent movement of Biharis. Banks looted. Young women raped and paraded naked before being shot dead. Dead bodies strewn all over the town. Many burnt alive. Some nailed up and shot dead. Surviving injured reported that mothers were made to drink the blood of their own children. Almost the whole of Bihari population wiped out. (About 15,000 killed.)
Pabna	23 MARCH– 10 APRIL Pabna Town	Awami League reign of terror continued for two weeks until the town secured by the Army. (About 200 killed.)
	23 MARCH– 10 APRIL Sirjganj	Miscreants lodged 350 men, women and children in a building and then set it on fire. (All inmates trapped and killed.)
	10 APRIL Paksey	Railway colony residents deceived under the pretext of forming Peace Committee, later confined in a High School building and burnt alive. (About 2,000 killed.)
Rangpur	23-31 MARCH Saidpur	Hundreds of houses burnt along with their inmates. (More than 100 people killed.)
	23 MARCH– 1 APRIL Nilphamari	More than half the refugee population of 5,000 was brutally massacred. (About 2,700 killed.)

AL Awami League EBR East Bengal Regiment EPR East Pakistan Rifles

District	Date (1971) Area	Incident
Dinajpur	28 MARCH– 1 APRIL Dinajpur Town	Atrocities began with the revolt of EBR, followed by mass killings. Men, women and children slaughtered. Only stray survivors consisted mainly of old women and children. Heads of victims were hung on tree tops. About 400 girls abducted to India. (About 5,000 killed.)
	28 MARCH– 13 APRIL Thakurgaon	EBR revolted and most of Bihari population wiped out. Young girls abducted. Women were raped and those pregnant bayoneted. Still-born babies torn to pieces. Corpses dragged naked along the streets. (About 3,000 killed.)
	Parbatipur, Ponchagarh, Chaur Kai Phulbari and Hilli	Railway colonies were the main target of rebel EPR and Awami League volunteers. Grenades, light machine guns and small arms were used to terrorise the residents before unleashing orgy of rape and murder. (Survivors estimate more than 5,000 victims.)
Rajshahi	28 MARCH– 16 APRIL Rajshahi Town	Police and EPR revolted. Indian infiltrators also joined in and started killing indiscriminately until Army secured the town on 16 April 1971. Massacres also reported from Natore and Sarda. (About 2,000 killed.)
	27 MARCH– 18 APRIL Nawabganj	Rebel EPR elements, supported by Indian infiltrators, broke open Nawabganj jail, released prisoners

AL Awami League EBR East Bengal Regiment EPR East Pakistan Rifles

District	Date (1971) Area	Incident
		and incited them to acts of violence and arson. An Accounts Clerk buried up to waist for refusing to accept 'Bangla Desh' and killed with cudgels. (Total deaths estimated at about 1,000.)
Comilla	MARCH-14 APRIL Brahmanbaria	Bihari men, women and children in Brahmanbaria rounded up and lodged in jail before being killed by automatic fire under orders of rebel Company Commander of EBR on 13 April, 1971. (Casualties approx. 500 killed.)
Mymensingh	27 MARCH Mymensingh Cantonment	EBR/EPR revolted and killed their West Pakistani colleagues, including Officers and men resting for the night in their residential quarters and barracks.
	16/17 APRIL Mymensingh Town	Ex-EPR personnel armed with machine guns, raided Mymensingh District Jail and shot 17 non-locals lodged there for safe custody.
	17-20 APRIL Shankipara and other colonies	Violent mobs, armed with rifles, swords, spears, daggers and sickles, attacked and killed the bulk of the male residents of Shankipara and nine other colonies in and around Mymensingh town. About 5,000 reported killed. Women collected in a mosque and a school building, later rescued by the Army when the town was secured on 21 April, 1971.

AL Awami League EBR East Bengal Regiment EPR East Pakistan Rifles

Appendix **8** Major events in the Pakistani Civil War,
November 1971 — January 1972

The smoldering situation in East Pakistan burst into full scale war at the end of 1971, with India coming to the aid of the Bengla Desh rebels, giving them the military assistance that enabled them to successfully fight the West Pakistani troops and establish the new nation of Bengla Desh. Below is a brief, chronological summary of major events in the War.

NOVEMBER 23 After weeks of border skirmishes between India and Pakistan, President Khan declared a State of National Emergency in Pakistan, paving the way for possible censorship, civilian mobilization, martial law and other measures. Khan charged that Indian troops had seized and held the East Pakistani villages of Chuagacha in Jessore, and Atgram in Sylhet, as well as several other border outposts. Air battles were fought over Jessore and Western India.

DECEMBER 3 Full scale war broke out between Pakistan and India. India accused Pakistan of having expanded fighting into major conflict by carrying out strikes against eight airfields in India. Prime Minister Indira Gandhi's Indian government recognized Bengla Desh as an independent nation. In retaliation for this act, Pakistan broke off diplomatic relations with India, although she had not done so during the Indian-Pakistani wars of 1948 and 1965.

DECEMBER 4 President Yahya Khan of Pakistan declared war on India.

DECEMBER 7 Indian troops captured Jessore, virtually assuring India's control over half of Eastern Pakistan.

DECEMBER 8 India announced that she had captured the East Pakistani cities of Comilla and Brahmanbaria, which are located close to the Eastern border of Pakistan. Comilla fell without offering resistance.

DECEMBER 9 300 children were killed when Indian aircraft bombed an orphanage in Dacca, East Pakistan.

DECEMBER 14 The entire East Pakistan government resigned, disassociating itself from future actions of Khan's Central Government.

DECEMBER 16 The War Ended. Pakistani forces surrendered to India. The Commander of the Pakistani Army, A.A.K. Nizia ceased fighting only five days after vowing that he would never capitulate.

DECEMBER 17 India and Pakistan signed a cease-fire agreement.

DECEMBER 20 President Khan resigned and was replaced by Bhutto, who ordered Khan placed under house arrest.

DECEMBER 21 Bhutto appointed Nurul Anin, A Bengali, Vice President of Western Pakistan. Bhutto also announced that Sheik Mujibir Rahman would be released from prison, where he had been under a sentence of death since March, 1971. Rahman was to be placed under house arrest.

DECEMBER 22 Foreign Minister Singh of Pakistan concedes "Reality" of the nation of Bengla Desh. Rahman was released from prison.

DECEMBER 27 Bhutto and Rahman met in Rawalpirdi.

JANUARY 1 First Bengali refugees returned to Bengla Desh from India.

JANUARY 3 Bhutto announced that Rahman would be unconditionally released from custody.

JANUARY 8 Rahman was freed from custody and, in a surprise move, flown to London, where he met with representatives of the press.

JANUARY 10 Rahman met in Delhi with Indira Ghandi, and then returned to Bengla Desh, where he assumed the post of Prime Minister in the new government.

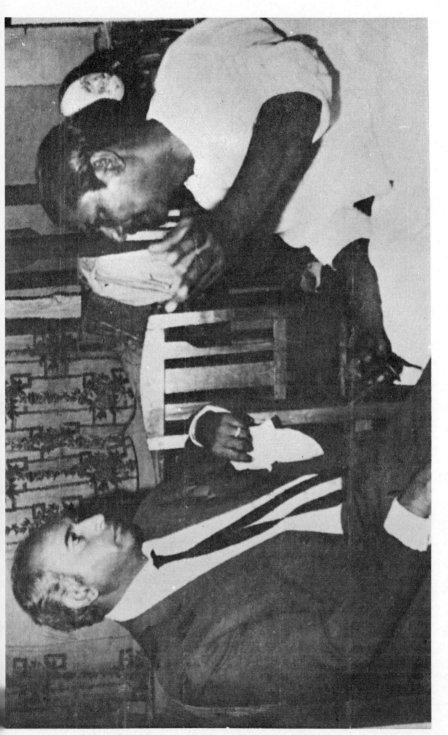

Z.A.Bhutto and Sheikh Mujibur Rehman (right) are shown meeting in February 1969 to discuss the mounting political crisis in East Pakistan

mer Pakistani President Yahya Khan, removed from
ice and placed under house arrest by Bhutto after
t Pakistan broke away in December, 1971

East Pakistani rebel soldiers on alert, June 1971

Rebel soldiers stare at bodies of Punjabi businessmen murdered by Bengali rebels as "alleged spies" for the Pakistani government in April, 1971

East Pakistani refugees huddle under plastic tents to keep out of the rain

Refugee Mother and Child

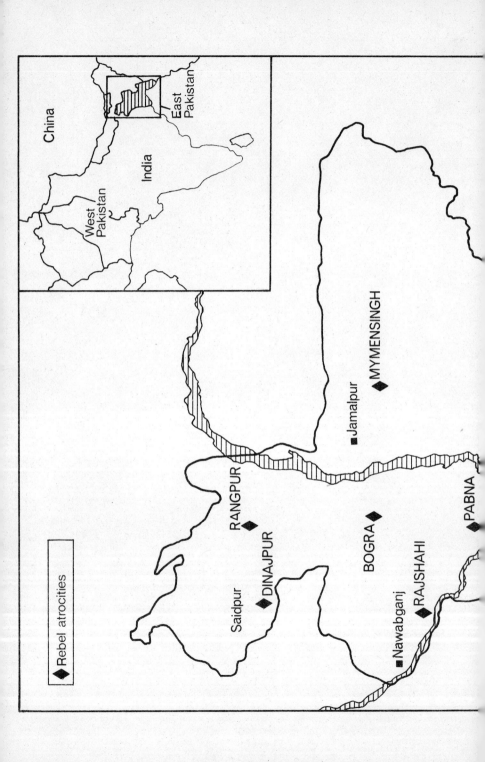

Rebel atrocities

China

West Pakistan

India

East Pakistan

RANGPUR

Saidpur

DINAJPUR

BOGRA

Nawabganj

RAJSHAHI

PABNA

Jamalpur

MYMENSINGH

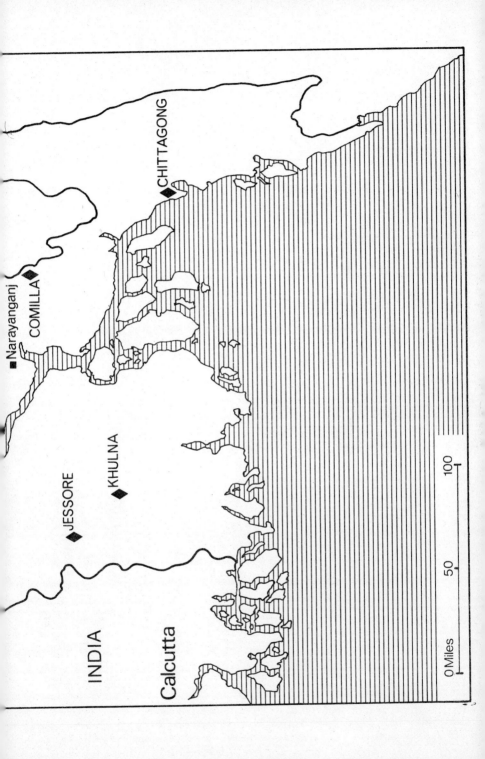